MW01131466

RETREAT THROUGH THE RHONE VALLEY

RETREAT THROUGH THE RHONE VALLEY

Defensive battles of the Nineteenth Army,
August–September 1944

JÖRG STAIGER

Translated by
LINDEN LYONS

Series editor:
MATTHIAS STROHN

CASEMATE

Philadelphia & Oxford

AN AUSA BOOK
Association of the United States Army
2425 Wilson Boulevard, Arlington, Virginia 22201, USA

Published in the United States of America and Great Britain in 2023 by
CASEMATE PUBLISHERS
1950 Lawrence Road, Havertown, PA 19083, USA
and
The Old Music Hall, 106–108 Cowley Road, Oxford OX4 1JE, UK

Originally published as Die Wehrmacht im Kampf Band 39: *Rückzug durchs Rhônetal: Abwehr-und Verzögerungskampf der 19. Armee im Herbst 1944 unter besonderer Berücksichtigung des Einsatzes der 11. Panzer-Division* (Neckargemünd: Scharnhorst Buchkameradschaft, 1965)

Hardback Edition: ISBN 978-1-63624-230-9
Digital Edition: ISBN 978-1-63624-231-6

A CIP record for this book is available from the British Library

Printed and bound in the United Kingdom by CPI Group (UK) Ltd, Croydon, CR0 4YY

Typeset in India by Lapiz Digital Services, Chennai.

For a complete list of Casemate titles, please contact:
CASEMATE PUBLISHERS (US)
Telephone (610) 853-9131
Fax (610) 853-9146
Email: casemate@casematepublishers.com
www.casematepublishers.com

CASEMATE PUBLISHERS (UK)
Telephone (0)1226 734350
Email: casemate-uk@casematepublishers.co.uk
www.casematepublishers.co.uk

Publisher's note: This text is a faithful translation of the original German and as such may include language that is now considered offensive.
Front cover: Troops of the 45th Division wade ashore near Ste. Maxime. (U.S. Army photo)

Contents

Introduction

This book covers the fighting and withdrawal of the German Nineteenth Army in southern France, following the Allied landings in Operation *Dragoon* in August 1944. This episode is one of the less known ones of the Second World War. Other campaigns have overshadowed the events that took place in southern France between August and September 1944. The reasons for this are obvious. The landings were hardly opposed, and the German forces, spread thin by a multi-front war, were no match for an enemy who could rely on overwhelming superiority in men and material. As a result, the fight did not last very long and the campaign was characterised by a rapid German withdrawal, which tried to save as many units and formations as possible. The desperate situation of the Germans shines throughout the pages of this book. Perhaps the most striking example of the paltry state of the Nineteenth Army can be found in a comment in the references, which states that German troops had to be transported to the front line in motorbuses powered by wood gas. The uncertainties and the 'fog of war' also played a role, as vividly explained by the author, Jörg Staiger, when he mentions the inability of the 11th Panzer Division to cross the river Drôme, which had swelled due to heavy rainfall.

Being able to cope with such unforeseeable problems in the face of an overwhelming enemy is, to put it mildly, a challenge for every military commander. In many ways, this underlying theme is the real essence of the book. It is not without reason that the author starts the opus by quoting from the *Truppenführung*, the German manual used in the Second World War. This manual has been called the most important piece of doctrine ever written and within it one finds the explanations for the success of the German Wehrmacht on the battlefield. Accepting the uncertainties of war was a core feature of this manual.

But restricting these insights to the Second World War would not fully grasp the importance of this book within the context of the time it was written. The German edition was published in 1965, when the Cold War was in full swing. This was also the time when strategic thinkers moved away from a doctrine of massive retaliation to flexible response, which was finally adopted in 1967. With this, more operational freedom was granted to NATO's formations, which also included some aspects of withdrawal and delaying resistance. The German withdrawal in southern France in the summer of 1944 offered valuable lessons for a fight against a potential enemy that had manpower and material, but lacked flexibility in thinking and actions. This might also explain why the actions of the French Forces of the Interior, basically the resistance movement, are hardly mentioned in the book, despite Staiger's comment that they had a considerable impact on German actions. In a Cold War scenario, fighting on NATO territory, a partisan movement against NATO troops was not part of the Western alliance's planning assumptions. Staiger clearly makes the point about the contemporary relevance in the conclusion when he states that the actions of 11th Panzer Division, in particular, would offer valuable lessons for the Army in 1965. Here, he also highlights one factor that should not be overlooked. When Staiger wrote the manuscript, not all files were available to him and some of the wider aspects of the book might not have stood the test of time. Some points, like the treatment of the civilian population or the already mentioned French Forces of the Interior, hardly feature in the book. In this sense, it is a classical operational study, one that presents and analyses military actions. In the light of more modern historiography, some might see this as an issue, but it is also the strength of this book which, by concentrating on the pure military aspects, helps us understand this under-studied campaign.

Matthias Strohn

Foreword

The retreat of the Nineteenth Army from the French Mediterranean coast to the Belfort Gap in August and September 1944 is particularly remarkable due to the fact that the combat formations, with the exception of the 11th Panzer Division, were severely lacking in what was regarded in *Truppenführung*, the field manual of the German Army, as the means by which such an operation could be carried out in an orderly manner.

Meanwhile, the enemy had everything he needed for the successful pursuit of the German forces, and he knew how to exploit the resources at his disposal with skill and foresight. That he nevertheless failed on two occasions to bring about the seemingly inevitable complete destruction of the Nineteenth Army was because of 'those unpredictable factors that often have a significant influence on events. Our own will comes up against the independent will of the enemy. Error and attrition are ordinary phenomena. Despite the role of technology in warfare, it is the individual worth of the soldier that remains decisive.'[1]

In memory of the dead on both sides.

Jörg Staiger

---

1   *Truppenführung*, Part I, paragraph 3.

Introduction

The subject of this study encompasses the principles for the following forms of combat that had been put down in writing in *Truppenführung*, the field manual of the German Army from 17 October 1933:

- Attack against positions – paragraphs 386–407
- Defence – paragraphs 427–437 and 596
- Withdrawal from action, retreat – paragraphs 503–530
- Pursuit – paragraphs 410–426

In comparing the measures taken by both sides, an attempt has been made to convey a vivid and comprehensive picture of the events that unfolded. Nevertheless, the wealth of material has made it necessary to summarise the conduct of operations so that the course of events will not be blurred by too many details of individual actions, interesting though they may be.

Allied air operations after the landing are not taken into consideration in this book. Air strikes were rarely carried out, as the Americans did not want to hinder their own advance by cratering the terrain whenever they bombed German defensive lines.

The activity of the French Forces of the Interior (FFI) is only referred to occasionally. The reader might conclude from this that the impact of the FFI on the conduct of operations was insignificant. Quite the opposite! The FFI had an influence on many tactical measures taken by the German military leadership, and its mere presence meant that it was difficult to gain an accurate picture of what the enemy was up to. As a result, the FFI was always a factor that had to be taken into account in any decision that had to be made.

For example, the FFI control over the French Jura Mountains meant that the Nineteenth Army could not simply continue its retreat along the road that ran through Bourg-en-Bresse, Lons-le-Saunier, Mouchard, and Besançon. It was necessary for this road to be cleared beforehand. And in carrying out its task of establishing a defensive line in the Montagnes du Lomont at the beginning of September 1944, the 61st Panzer Reconnaissance Battalion first had to clear the roads leading from Montbéliard to the south.

Only once the Vosges Position had been reached did the constant danger posed by the FFI disappear.

CHAPTER I

Operation *Anvil/Dragoon* and German defensive measures along the French Mediterranean coast

The situation of the Nineteenth Army at the beginning of August 1944

On 2 July 1944, General of Infantry Friedrich Wiese took over command of the Nineteenth Army from General of Infantry Georg von Sodenstern. The Nineteenth Army was subordinate to Army Group G (Colonel-General Johannes Blaskowitz), which was responsible for the defence of the southern French coast between Menton on the Italian frontier and Cerbère on the Spanish.

The battle in Normandy had by then been raging for almost four weeks. The landing there had taken place on 6 June. Three of the most well-equipped infantry divisions (the 271st, 272nd, and 277th) and four army artillery battalions (the 1192nd, 1193rd, 1194th, and 1198th) had been detached from the Nineteenth Army and committed to the fighting in Normandy. Barely any replacements could be allocated to the Nineteenth Army, which meant that it would be difficult for it to carry out the defensive tasks with which it had been entrusted. The objections raised by the headquarters of the Nineteenth Army were of no avail, for the Führer had explicitly ordered that 'forces are to be sent to Normandy even from sectors that appear to be in danger'.

At the end of July, the Nineteenth Army had to hand over the 9th Panzer Division to the front in Normandy. This formation had been in position to the north-west of Marseille and had been fully prepared to go into battle. With its departure, the Nineteenth Army would be devoid of any mobile reserve. Even in the entire combat zone of Army Group G, there was only one mobile strike formation that remained in reserve. That formation was the 11th Panzer Division, which had assembled in the Caillac–Toulouse–Carcassonne–Albi area in readiness for action with the First Army near the Bay of Biscay or with the Nineteenth Army along the Mediterranean front.

General of Artillery Walter Warlimont, the deputy chief of the operations staff of the High Command of the Wehrmacht (OKW), visited the front in southern France in the spring of 1944. He had prepared several recommendations for the conduct of battle in the event of an enemy landing on the French Mediterranean coast. These ranged from the defence of the coast to the withdrawal of the front to a position near the Swiss frontier, where the alpine passes leading to Italy could be interdicted.

If the enemy were to conduct a landing operation in the Mediterranean combat zone, his most probable attack objectives would be the port cities of Marseille and Toulon on the French coast and Genoa on the Italian. However, directives for the action to be taken in the event of such an operation were issued to neither Army Group C in northern Italy nor Army Group G in southern France. Discussions between the headquarters of the two army groups failed to achieve anything.

At a conference that took place on 11 July between the leadership of Army Group G and that of the Nineteenth Army, it was concluded that any seaborne landing by the Allies would encompass the mouth of the Rhône as well as the city of Marseille, and that this would be accompanied by airborne landings in the Camargue and the Crau, both of which were regions near the city of Arles. However, it was not just the coastal sector between the mouth of the Rhône and the city of Marseille that was regarded as being in danger; so too was that between the city of Toulon and the Gulf of Fréjus.

The headquarters of the Nineteenth Army requested, quite logically, that the 11th Panzer Division be moved to the former assembly area of the 9th Panzer Division north of Marseille. Unfortunately, Army Group G was unable to grant this request. The 11th Panzer Division had been placed under the direct command of the OKW, and Colonel-General Alfred Jodl, the chief of the operations staff of the OKW, did not consider it an opportune moment to seek Hitler's approval on this matter.

It was pointed out by the headquarters of the Nineteenth Army that the 11th Panzer Division would arrive too late to counteract an enemy landing in the vicinity of Marseille if it were to remain in its current assembly area. Due to the shortage of means of transportation of heavy equipment, elements of the panzer division would need to be brought to the front by rail. It could be expected that the French Forces of the Interior (FFI) would step up their attacks against railway lines in the event of an enemy landing operation, which meant that there would be no time during which the security of rail transport could be guaranteed. The Nineteenth Army estimated that it would take approximately 24 hours for half of the tracked vehicles of the panzer division to reach the front by road. Despite these concerns, the panzer division stayed where it was.

At the beginning of August 1944, the forces of the Nineteenth Army were organised for defensive action as follows:

- LXII Reserve Corps between the Italian frontier and Toulon with:
  - 148th Reserve Division
  - 242nd Infantry Division (static formation predominantly based in Toulon)
  - Strength approximately 21,000 men
- LXXXV Army Corps (formerly Group Knieß) between Toulon and Montpellier with:
  - 244th Infantry Division (static formation based in Marseille)
  - 338th Infantry Division (static formation)
  - Strength approximately 19,000 men
- IV Luftwaffe Field Corps between Montpellier and the Spanish frontier with:
  - 189th Reserve Division
  - 198th Infantry Division
  - 716th Infantry Division (remnants)
  - Strength approximately 19,000 men

These forces were woefully insufficient for the defence of a coastal sector of 500 kilometres as the crow flies, even when taking into consideration the German naval and air units that had been committed to the area. Marseille and Toulon alone, both of which had been declared as fortresses with fronts facing towards sea and land, tied down one and a half infantry divisions firmly to their defence.

Although the construction of the Mediterranean Wall had resumed at the beginning of 1944, it encompassed not the entire coast but rather only focal points like Marseille, Toulon, and the Gulf of Fréjus. The army formations that had been committed to the coast lacked the men and materiel needed to set up beach obstacles and field fortifications in the intermediary sectors. On top of this, the terrain further inland urgently needed to be reinforced for defence against airborne landings.

Much had been done by the beginning of July 1944, but the German experience in Normandy made it utterly clear that the Mediterranean Wall would be incapable of holding out against a serious landing operation conducted by the enemy. In assessing the operational readiness of the positional divisions, it ought to be remembered that six of our battalions were composed of soldiers from the occupied regions in the East. There was in particular a large percentage of non-citizen ethnic Germans. Furthermore, it should be borne in mind that none of our formations had any major combat experience.

Because our army artillery was unable to cover the entire coast with fire, it was necessary that French coastal artillery units, which had been requisitioned by our navy, as well as flak units be employed. Nevertheless, there remained long stretches of the coast, especially between Toulon and the Italian border, that remained outside the range of our fire.

An artillery exercise in the middle of July in the fortress area of Toulon revealed significant deficiencies in the signal communications of our artillery units. Lacking in mobility, these units could not quickly concentrate their fire. The static infantry divisions were equipped with Russian, French, and Italian artillery pieces. They were low on stocks of ammunition and therefore enjoyed few opportunities to conduct exercises. Despite these problems, of which the operations staff of the Wehrmacht was fully aware, Hitler ordered on 13 August that 'the coastline is to be defended'.

Cooperation with the navy in the planning and carrying out of preparatory defensive measures was unsatisfactory. The headquarters of the Nineteenth Army could only make suggestions to Naval District

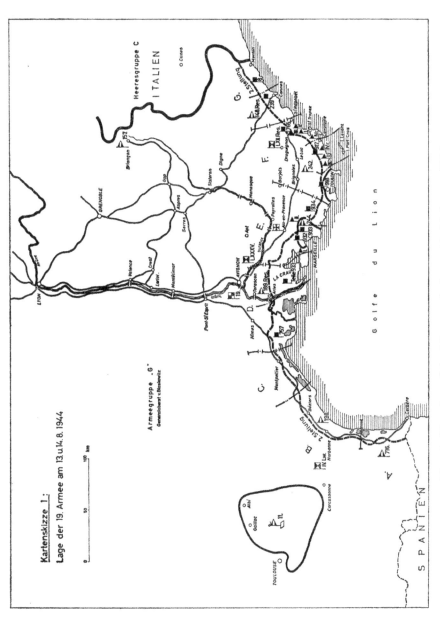

Map 1: Situation of the Nineteenth Army, 13–14 August 1944

Southern France, the result of which was the lack of coordination of all available defensive forces. The inexpediency of the different spheres of military authority is demonstrated by a conference which took place with the navy in Marseille on 25 June. The army headquarters emphasised on that occasion that the port installations in Marseille could not under any circumstances be allowed to fall into the hands of the enemy intact in the event of a landing there, and therefore recommended that they be blown up at once. The navy rejected this suggestion, as it required the large port in Marseille for servicing not only the 6th Security Flotilla, which at that time comprised six small vessels, but also several ambulance ships and Swiss merchantmen. It was also where building materials were transshipped for Organisation Todt. In any case, the navy had not been given permission to destroy the port. The only agreement that was reached in the end was to destroy nine smaller ports along the southern French coast and partially block the port entrances in Marseille.

It was not just the handing over of troops to the front in Normandy that caused the headquarters of the Nineteenth Army great concern; so too did the combat activity of the French Resistance movement, which had been increasing in intensity ever since the Allied invasion of mainland Europe. The few reserves available in the rear area, especially in the combat zones of the LXII Reserve Corps and the LXXXV Army Corps, were tied down constantly to operations against the FFI, which the Allies systematically supplied by air with weapons, equipment, and additional personnel. From June onwards, these bloody operations cost approximately 1,000 men per month. Furthermore, it was clear from the reports provided by informants that the FFI had been instructed to create regular combat formations. The Nineteenth Army could therefore expect that enemy forces whose strength was not to be underestimated would appear to the rear in the event of a landing, and that those forces would attempt above all else to disrupt the flow of supplies through the valley of the Rhône.

The enemy intensified his air strikes throughout July. His primary objectives were the destruction of the bridges across the Rhône near and to the south of Avignon and the disruption of road and rail traffic leading to Italy. By the end of the month, the main bridges across the

Rhône had been so damaged by bombs from the air that it would take several days and even weeks for them to be repaired. With each day that went by, it became more difficult for our troops to cross the river. Anti-aircraft defences in the combat zone of the Nineteenth Army were reduced in strength when elements of the light and medium battalions of the 5th Flak Brigade accompanied the 2nd Air Division in its shift to new airfields further to the north. The Nineteenth Army itself had no army flak battalions at its disposal.

The navy, which, aside from the Luftwaffe, was the most important branch of the Wehrmacht for the conduct of reconnaissance, took the decision to withdraw some of its security boats in July. The reason for this decision was an increase in enemy naval activity along the coast between Toulon and the Italian frontier, the result of which had been the loss of several security boats.

On 4 August, Army Group G submitted to the German Army Command in the West (OB West) its assessment of the situation in the combat zone of the Nineteenth Army. It was clearly pointed out in this assessment that the Nineteenth Army would no longer be capable of coping with the task it had originally been given:

> Commander of Army Group G
> Ia No. 1598/44
> Headquarters, 4 August 1944
>
> Re: Situation of the Nineteenth Army
>
> To OB West
>
> At the beginning of the invasion of Normandy, the Nineteenth Army was still in a condition to repel landings on the Mediterranean coast or, if such landings were successful, to hurl the enemy back in the water with a counter-attack.
> In the course of the last few weeks, the Nineteenth Army has been deprived of the following formations:
>
> - 277th Infantry Division
> - 272nd Infantry Division
> - 271st Infantry Division
> - 341st Assault Gun Brigade
> - Four motorised army artillery battalions

- Four personnel replacement transfer battalions (earmarked for the 352nd Infantry Division, but never arrived)
- Personnel Replacement Transfer Battalion G1 (1,280 men)
- 989th Heavy Artillery Battalion (which was to be refreshed and refitted in the combat zone of the 716th Infantry Division)

Detached from the reserve forces of the Nineteenth Army were the following formations:

- Headquarters of the LVIII Panzer Corps
- 2nd SS Panzer Division Das Reich
- 9th SS Panzer Division Hohenstaufen

The 394th Assault Gun Brigade had been promised but never arrived, while one personnel replacement transfer battalion from the 148th Reserve Division was used to replenish the 716th Infantry Division.

To replace the formations that had been handed over, the Nineteenth Army was given the following:

- 198th Infantry Division
- 716th Infantry Division (of which there were only battered remnants)
- Four personnel replacement transfer battalions (without weapons)
- Elements of the 189th Reserve Division
- One anti-tank artillery battalion

Given the situation in the combat zone of Army Group B, the headquarters of Army Group G fully understands the necessity of diverting forces from the Nineteenth Army. Nevertheless, it must be pointed out that the reduced numbers of men and weapons has so weakened the defensive strength of the Nineteenth Army that it can no longer be expected to be able to defend the coast with any degree of success.

Army Group G is making every effort, with all the means at its disposal, to improve the power of resistance of the Nineteenth Army. It will continue to do so even if further forces are detached from the Nineteenth Army. This report is submitted to OB West so that the conclusions to be drawn can be agreed upon.

Signed Blaskowitz

Meanwhile, enemy aerial activity increased steadily from day to day. These air raids, in connection with intelligence reports, indicated that an enemy landing would soon take place either in the vicinity of Genoa or somewhere on the French Mediterranean coast. While the Reich Foreign Ministry, based on the information it had received, anticipated a landing in Italy, the army and the navy, aware of the fact that all French formations had been withdrawn from the Italian front, held the opinion that the landing would be carried out on the French Mediterranean coast in the Marseille–Toulon sector. A landing on the coast of the Bay of Biscay was no longer an issue, especially because the American envelopment attack from Normandy towards the east would make it necessary for the Allied leadership to secure the port in Marseille for the delivery of supplies.

Given this assessment of the situation, the headquarters of Army Group G decided that the 11th Panzer Division ought to be temporarily committed to the combat zone of the Nineteenth Army. On 9 August, in accordance with this decision, the Nineteenth Army issued its Order No. 14:

> Headquarters of the Nineteenth Army, 9 August 1944
> Ia No. 81/10/44
>
> Re: Commitment of the 11th Panzer Division against enemy landings on the French Mediterranean coast
>
> Army Order No. 14
>
> 1. The 11th Panzer Division, stationed in the Caillac–Toulouse–Carcassonne–Albi area, will be placed under the command of the Nineteenth Army at the onset of combat action on the French Mediterranean coast.
> 2. It is possible for the panzer division, from its current standby area, to conduct the following operations:
> (a) A counter-attack in the direction of Narbonne.
> (b) A counter-attack in the direction of Agde and Sète via Béziers.
> Following the assembly of the panzer division near Nîmes or south of Avignon, the following operations will also be possible:
> (c) A counter-attack towards the south through the Camargue on the west bank of the Rhône or through the Crau on the east bank of the river in the direction of the Gulf of Fos.
> (d) A counter-attack in the direction of Marseille or Toulon.
> 3. Preparations are to be made for the occupation of the second position in the Lunel–Arles–Orgon sector or of the switch position on either side of Carcassonne by those elements of the panzer division, reinforced with various troops and standby units, which remain immobile. Documents relating to the second position can be obtained from the pioneer officer at the headquarters

of the Nineteenth Army and those relating to the switch position from the headquarters of the IV Luftwaffe Field Corps.

4. The 11th Panzer Division is to establish contact with the IV Luftwaffe Field Corps, under whose command it will probably be placed in cases 2a and 2b, as soon as possible.

5. Any operations yet to be conducted are to be preceded by thorough reconnaissance. Map exercises should also be carried out and clear orders issued by formation and unit commanders. The panzer division will report as soon as possible which roads it will take in its advance from its current standby area to its assembly area.

6. The signal officer at the headquarters of the Nineteenth Army shall establish radio contact with the headquarters of the 11th Panzer Division. This will ensure that the conduct of operations by the panzer division can be controlled by radio.

7. Preparations are to be made by the senior quartermaster at the headquarters of the Nineteenth Army for the supply of the 11th Panzer Division for the operations listed above. If it has not already done so, the panzer division is to inform the senior quartermaster of its supply requirements as soon as possible.

Special orders for the supply units will follow.

On 10 August, when the first reports arrived of the putting to sea of large convoys from Italian and North African ports, the defensive power of the Nineteenth Army was further reduced. OB West ordered that the 338th Infantry Division, without any other formation available to replace it, be detached and allocated to Army Group B. In addition, three anti-tank companies, amounting to 24 tractor-drawn 7.5-centimetre guns, were to be transferred to Paris.

Given the reports of approaching enemy convoys, the Nineteenth Army immediately requested that it be allowed to retain the 338th Infantry Division for the time being. This request was rejected by OB West, and the departure of the 338th Infantry Division commenced on 11 August.

On 11 and 12 August, the enemy intensified his air raids along the coastal sector between Marseille and the Italian frontier and against the bridges across the Rhône. Radar installations belonging to the Luftwaffe and the navy were specifically targeted, and so too were our battery positions. At 0800 hours on 12 August, our aerial reconnaissance reported that two convoys, each with 70–100 ships and aircraft carriers, were steering for the Bay of Ajaccio in Corsica. It was clear to those at the headquarters of Army Group G and at that of the Nineteenth Army that a landing on the French Mediterranean coast was imminent. The report that was immediately passed on to the OKW compelled Colonel-General Jodl to present to Hitler the orders that had been drafted to deal with the possibility of a landing on the French Mediterranean coast. Hitler decided on Order No. 3, 'Defence of the Coast', and approved the release of the 11th Panzer Division for action in the combat zone of the Nineteenth Army. The army group, at noon on 13 August, was therefore able to give the panzer division the order to move to a position on either side of the Rhône. In particular, a panzer battle group was to assemble to the east of the river.

Despite the fact that this urgently needed reinforcement of the Nineteenth Army had been approved, its belatedness meant that the panzer division would be unable to arrive in time to intervene against the enemy landing at the moment of its greatest weakness, regardless of whether this landing was to take place to the east or west of the Rhône.

★ ★ ★

The Nineteenth Army had taken several measures in preparation for the imminent defensive battle. In addition to issuing orders to the corps in relation to the conduct of reconnaissance and the creation of a defensive focal point, such measures included setting up supply depots, signposting roads, posting maintenance units of Organisation Todt at bridge sites, and assigning city commandants to the most important cities and rail commandants to the railway lines. The commander of the Nineteenth Army himself tirelessly oversaw these preparations and was always ready to provide advice, offer help, and issue orders. What remains unanswered is whether the Rhône crossings had received the attention they truly needed from our pioneer units. Had it never been considered that on X-Day, the day of the landing, there would not be a single bridge across the Rhône between Lyon and Arles that would be in a condition to be used? The pioneer officer at the headquarters of the Nineteenth Army had seen to the consolidation of the road bridges across the Rhône at Tarascon, Arles, and Saint-Gilles and across the Durance at Avignon, increasing their load-bearing capacity to 70 tonnes, and had stationed construction units of Organisation Todt, equipped with repair material, in the vicinity of the bridges, but the only other means of crossing the rivers that were available were three 12-tonne ferries at Avignon and one 30-tonne ferry at Arles. There is no indication from currently accessible documents that any measures had been taken to enable the crossing of the rivers by the heavy vehicles and equipment of the 11th Panzer Division.

In order to properly put into context the performance of the troops in the fighting that followed, it should be strongly emphasised that the strength of our formations and the equipment at their disposal were by no means sufficient for the combat tasks that would need to be carried out. This was especially the case for our infantry and artillery formations. There was a shortage everywhere of infantry weapons and pioneer equipment. Only a handful of infantry battalions could be moved quickly by bicycle or bus, while our artillery units, if not static, were predominantly horse-drawn, with only a few batteries temporarily able to be moved through motorised power. Even the 5th Flak Brigade, 30 per cent of which comprised personnel of the Reich Labour Service (RAD), was only partially motorised, which meant that its elements could only be moved from one location to another bit by bit.

The enemy enjoyed complete and nonstop aerial superiority. At the time of the enemy landing, there was a total of 185 German aircraft in the Mediterranean theatre of operations. This small number would be unable to make any meaningful impact. For days on end, the Nineteenth Army had no means whatsoever of being able to conduct aerial reconnaissance.

Not to remain unmentioned was the strong revival of the resistance movement in France which coincided with the commencement of the Allied landing. The nervousness and uncertainty caused by the disruptions to German troop movements further inland could not be underestimated.

Allied planning for Operation Anvil/Dragoon

The landing on the French Mediterranean coast had been agreed upon by Roosevelt, Stalin, and Churchill during the Tehran Conference at the end of November 1943 and was scheduled to take place at the same time as the invasion of Normandy. This plan did not correspond to the original train of thought of Churchill, who would have preferred to see put into effect his operational recommendation of a breakthrough from

Italy in the direction of Yugoslavia, Hungary, and Austria, as it was his hope that such an operation would keep the Russians out of much of Europe.

Standing in the way of Churchill's operational plan were the extraordinarily difficult geographical challenges that would be involved. Aside from this, the Americans were not yet interested in Churchill's political considerations for the post-war era. However, a point in favour of his idea was the inadequate number of ships available for the conduct of simultaneous landings of sufficient strength in Normandy and on the French Mediterranean coast.

In March 1944, despite all objections, the Combined Chiefs of Staff decided to go ahead with Operation *Anvil/Dragoon*. The date of the operation was set for approximately two months after the landing in Normandy, for it would be possible by then to have the ships needed for its conduct ready in the Mediterranean. Taking possession of the transshipment ports in Toulon and Marseille and establishing control over the rail, road, and water networks in the valley of the Rhône would be of prime importance for the Allied landing on the French Mediterranean coast.

When Lieutenant-General Omar N. Bradley, the commander of the US 12th Army Group, took the decision at the beginning of August 1944 not, as planned, to proceed with the conquest of Brittany and the seizure of its ports but rather to advance to the east in a wide arc, Operation *Anvil/Dragoon* became an absolute must.

Towards the end of 1943, following the agreement that had been made in Tehran, the first directives for Operation *Anvil*, which would be renamed *Dragoon* shortly before its execution, were issued to the commanders in chief in the Mediterranean theatre of operations. Initial planning was carried out by the US Fifth Army (Lieutenant-General Mark W. Clark) from January 1944 and then by the US Seventh Army (Major-General Alexander Patch) from March. In mid-April, the French approached the Combined Chiefs of Staff, which was carrying out its work in the vicinity of Algiers. Brigadier-General Charles de Gaulle insisted on cooperation and made it clear that, once the invasion of France was underway, French units would only be allowed to be committed to combat in the Motherland. He also invoked French honour to demand that French troops only be led by French commanders.

After the occupation of Rome on 7 June 1944, the US VI Corps – with the US 3rd, 36th, and 45th Infantry Divisions under its command – was pulled out of the front and transferred to the Naples–Salerno area so that it could prepare for the landing operation on the French Mediterranean coast. The French forces earmarked for participation in Operation *Anvil*, which consisted of two corps with seven divisions led by Army General Jean de Lattre de Tassigny, assembled near the ports of Taranto, Brindisi, and Oran. It was envisioned that the US VI Corps would carry out the landing and form a beachhead, while the French forces would land on about the third day and strike Toulon and Marseille. At the same time as this seaborne landing, an airborne landing of divisional strength was to take place in the vicinity of Draguignan and Le Muy so that the landing sector of the Gulf of Fréjus and Saint-Raphaël could be forced open from inland.

Once Marseille was taken, it was planned that Allied forces would advance in the direction of Lyon and Vichy.

The stretch of coast from the Bay of Cavalaire to Saint-Tropez and further to the Gulf of Fréjus was chosen as the landing sector. Any thought of a landing at Marseille and Toulon was rejected, as the German defences there, especially in terms of coastal artillery, were known to be too strong.

Although the coastal sector between Cavalaire and Fréjus had only a small number of sandy beaches that could be employed for the purposes of a landing operation, Allied intelligence on the terrain there was quite outstanding. The enemy possessed details of every metre of ground and was aware of the location of all German defensive installations right down to the last machine-gun nest.

There was a good road network in the landing sector. Two well-built roads led inland from the Cannes–Marseille coastal road, the first being Route Napoleon from Fréjus to Le Muy and the second the road from Cogolin across the moorland to Le Luc. Aside from that, there were many other smaller roads that led across the moorland and that were good enough for troop movements.

The US Army, Navy, and Air Force frequently disagreed on questions of detail in the planning of the landing. Even the US Seventh Army and US VI Corps initially held different views as to how the corps would best be employed. By 29 June, however, an agreement on how to proceed had been reached, and, on 18 July, the US Seventh Army issued its final orders for the landing. It would in fact be the first seaborne landing to be carried out by Allied forces in broad daylight.

To be committed to the landing operation, from left to right, were the following formations:

- US 3rd Infantry Division, commanded by Major-General John W. O'Daniel, with the US 7th and 15th Infantry Regiments making up the first wave for the landing on Alpha Beach between Cavalaire and Pampelonne, and the US 30th Infantry Regiment being placed in reserve behind the 7th Infantry Regiment
- US 45th Infantry Division, commanded by Major-General William W. Eagles, with the US 157th and 180th Infantry Regiments making up the first wave for the landing on Delta Beach between the Bay of Bougnon and La Nartelle, and the US 179th Infantry Regiment being placed in reserve in the centre
- US 36th Infantry Division, commanded by Major-General John E. Dahlquist, with the US 142nd, 143rd, and 141st Infantry Regiments making up the first wave for the landing on Camel Beach near Saint-Raphaël and Fréjus

French assault units would be employed on each wing of the landing sector. Their task would be to disrupt the flow of traffic along the coastal road and destroy the German artillery positions on the flanks.

The US-Canadian First Special Service Force would be sent into action against the German garrison on the island of Port-Cros, which lay in the vicinity of the left wing of the landing sector. Its objective would be the destruction of the 16.4-centimetre battery that was reported to be in position there so that the threat of flanking fire against the US 3rd Infantry Division could be eliminated.

Comprising the Allied 1st Airborne Task Force of US Major-General Robert T. Frederick were the British 2nd Independent Parachute Brigade, the US 517th Parachute Regimental Combat Team, the US 509th and 551st Parachute Infantry Battalions, the US 550th Glider Infantry Battalion, the US 460th and 463rd Parachute Field Artillery Battalions, the US 602nd Glider Pack Howitzer Battalion, and a number of supply units.

The task of the Allied 1st Airborne Task Force was to parachute its troops into the area of Draguignan and Le Muy four hours ahead of the seaborne landings and take Saint-Raphaël and Fréjus from inland in conjunction with the US 36th Infantry Division from the sea. The latter formation was scheduled to land two hours after both divisions to its left had done so.

Thirty-five days before the seaborne landing was to take place, the Allied air forces had been given the order to commence intensive strikes against German supply centres, supply roads, and defensive installations. Air strikes were to be concentrated against Marseille a day before the landing in order to make the German leadership believe that was where the landing would be carried out.

Aerial support on the day of the landing would commence at daybreak and would last until a point 30 minutes before the landing was to get underway at 0800 hours. 300 fighter-bombers were to conduct strikes against German coastal reinforcements, while 450 medium and heavy bombers, in waves of 40 heavy or 120 medium bombers, were to carpet-bomb the landing sectors.

At 0800 hours on X-Day, after massive preparatory fire by naval artillery and rocket ships, the US VI Corps was to land and push towards objectives on what had been designated the Blue Line.

On approximately X+1, both French corps under the command of General Lattre de Tassigny were to land behind the US VI Corps near Saint-Tropez. After assembling their forces, the French would advance in the direction of Toulon and Marseille and thereby relieve, as quickly as possible, the US 3rd Infantry Division, which would until that point be holding a line of security facing towards Toulon.

It was anticipated by the Allies that the German defence would be conducted similarly to that at the Anzio–Nettuno beachhead; specifically, that the landing would be met with delaying action, the purpose of which would be to gain time for the German military leadership to bring forward reserves.

Allied military intelligence estimated that the landing would be opposed by approximately 10 German infantry battalions, 50 tanks, 84 guns, and 14 self-propelled guns. This amounted to roughly one and a half infantry divisions on the day of the landing. It was expected that there would be two divisions at the front by X+1 and five by X+4, amongst them a full panzer division with approximately 200 tanks.

Preventing such an assembly of German forces opposite the beachhead was an important objective that had been set by Major-General Lucian K. Truscott, the commander of the US VI Corps. He had gained extensive experience of the consequences of such a development when he had been the commander of the US 3rd Infantry Division during the landing near Anzio and Nettuno. He wanted as many forces and as many heavy weapons as possible to land and reach the Blue Line quickly and then advance further. It was with this in mind that he, without any orders on the part of the US Seventh Army, intended to commit a motorised battle group – designated Task Force Butler – to a rapid advance along the Durance towards Aix or towards the north, with the objective of immediately disrupting any assembly of German forces in the vicinity of Aix or, in the event of a German retreat along the valley of the Rhône, of cutting off the route of retreat by occupying the town of Montélimar.

Since the US Seventh Army did not have any troops to place at the disposal of Task Force Butler, Major-General Truscott had to draw on motorised units that were already under the command of the US VI Corps. Once activated, the task force comprised one tank battalion, one armoured field artillery battalion, one tank destroyer company, one motorised infantry battalion, one engineer battalion, and the corps reconnaissance platoon. After the landing, the task force, under the command of Brigadier-General Frederick B. Butler, was to assemble and make itself ready as quickly as possible.

Lessons learned from the experience in Normandy extensively informed the preparations made for the landing. Following the conclusion

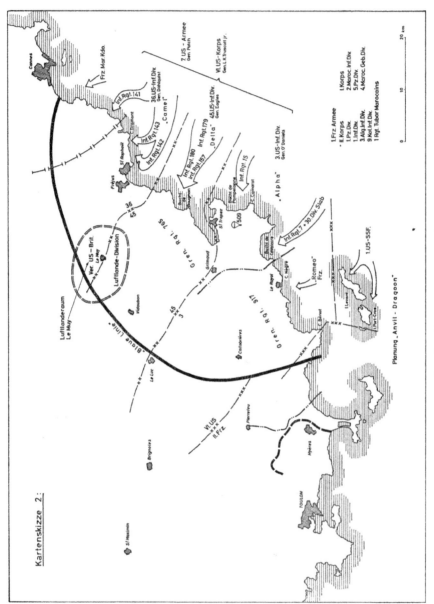

Map 2: The plan for Operation *Anvil/Dragoon*

of exercises on 7 August, the headquarters of the US Seventh Army and that of the US VI Corps were convinced that everything humanly possible had been done to prepare for and ensure the success of the landing.

The landing, 15–17 August 1944

(a) The attacker

At 2218 hours on 14 August, the landing fleet, consisting of a total of 1,200 ships and initially heading for Genoa with the idea of deceiving the German leadership, changed course and made for the French Mediterranean coast. Shortly afterwards, the Allied 1st Airborne Task Force took off from its 10 airfields near Rome with 396 aircraft and approximately 5,000 men. At 0455 hours, in the early-morning haze of dawn, the French coast came into view of the landing fleet.

The seaborne landing proceeded largely according to plan. The German coastal defences had been so shattered by carpet bombing between 0550 and 0730 hours, and by naval artillery fire from 0606 hours, that no serious resistance could be offered by the time the first troops sprang out of the landing boats at 0800 hours.

Only at Saint-Raphaël did everything not go according to plan, for mine clearance in the Gulf of Fréjus had been prevented by German defensive fire. The US 142nd Infantry Regiment was therefore unable to land in the sector that had been intended for it and had to be redirected to the sector of the US 143rd Infantry Regiment.

Despite the presence of ground fog, the Allied 1st Airborne Task Force conducted the airborne landing from 0315 hours in the designated area. By 0900 hours, 71 troop-carrying gliders had already landed. A navigational error resulted in the US 509th Parachute Infantry Battalion being unloaded over the peninsula of Saint-Tropez, and many of the paratroopers fell into the sea.

Of the two French assault operations, only that on the left wing, at Cape Nègre, enjoyed success. On the right wing, the French forces ran into a German minefield and, suffering heavy casualties, made no progress.

By the evening of 15 August, all three American divisions had reached, and in some locations had even pushed beyond, the Blue Line; 33,000 men, with 3,000 vehicles, had landed, while 2,000 German troops had been taken prisoner, and many more had been killed in action. Meanwhile, the Americans lost no more than 183 men.

German resistance had been surprisingly weak. The US Seventh Army therefore, as early as 16 August, authorised the continuation of the attack from the beachhead by the US VI Corps. It saw no need to await the landing of the two French corps.

In accordance with this authorisation, the US VI Corps ordered the US 3rd Infantry Division, minus the US 7th Infantry Regiment, to advance along Highway N-7 through Brignoles towards Saint-Maximin and to interdict all roads leading from Toulon. Meanwhile, the US 7th Infantry Regiment was to hold the Carnoules–Hyères line until relieved by French forces.

Immediately to the right of the US 3rd Infantry Division, the US 45th Infantry Division was to advance along a line through Vidauban, Salernes, Barjols, Rians, and Peyrolles.

The Allied 1st Airborne Task Force relieved the US 36th Infantry Division on the east flank of the beachhead. The latter formation assembled in the vicinity of Draguignan and Le Muy in readiness to push to the north-west (in the direction of Digne) or to the west. Task Force Butler had assembled near Le Muy by 17 August in preparation for further utilisation.

On 17 August, the first news arrived of the movement of the German 11th Panzer Division. It appeared as if it had been assigned the task of holding the American assault in check at Brignoles. However, this news did not induce the US VI Corps to revise the attack orders it had issued. The corps headquarters considered its forces strong enough to be able to resist those of the panzer division, and it had also become clear that the German leadership did not intend to draw on troops from Toulon who could have been employed to check the American advance.

On the evening of 17 August, the US VI Corps gave Task Force Butler, which had completed the assembly of its troops in the vicinity of Le Muy, the order to set off at 0600 hours on 18 August. The task force was to seize Montélimar and thereby cut off the route of retreat of German forces along the road beside the Rhône.

The initial objective would be Digne. In cooperation with the French Maquis, all roads leading from the west to the Digne–Grenoble highway were to be blocked.

The FFI proved to be a valuable ally for the Americans by engaging German troops in several skirmishes. It also provided intelligence on German forces, information on the terrain, support for American reconnaissance units, and assistance in setting up and manning roadblocks. Cooperation on a larger tactical scale did not come about, as the FFI had neither the required equipment nor the necessary command and organisational structure.

It was the intention of the US VI Corps that, once the valley of the Rhône had been reached at Montélimar, the encirclement and annihilation of all retreating German forces of the Nineteenth Army on the east bank of the river be carried out. Given that Task Force Butler would be too weak to lunge as far as Montélimar on its own, the corps, as early as the evening of 18 August, gave the order to the US 36th Infantry Division to follow the task force, which had already reached Sisteron that day.

Brigadier-General Butler would therefore have to wait a day in Sisteron and merely have his task force conduct reconnaissance in the direction of Montélimar and the high ground to its north. Only after that could he, together with the US 36th Infantry Division, lead his troops to the valley of the Rhône and see to it that the route of retreat of the German forces was cut off permanently.

Because the retreat order from the OKW only reached the headquarters of the German Nineteenth Army on 18 August, the US VI Corps had a head start of two full days for reaching Montélimar and setting up a defensive line.

(b) The defender

At 1815 hours on 14 August, German aerial reconnaissance reported that more than 100 enemy vessels, organised into two convoys, had put out to sea from the Bay of Ajaccio and had set course for the north-west. The headquarters of the Nineteenth Army thereupon informed the three corps under its command that a landing on the French southern coast could be expected on the night of 14/15 August. The IV Luftwaffe Field Corps received the order to prepare for the detachment of the 198th Infantry Division and to send the 305th Grenadier Regiment by truck at once to the area of Saint-Gilles, where it was to be placed in army reserve. The Nineteenth Army also requested of OB West that it be allowed to hold on to the 338th Infantry Division, for the 11th Panzer Division would be unable to arrive at the front in time.

The evaluation of the aerial reconnaissance report on the putting out to sea of the two convoys revealed that the armada could arrive near Marseille or the French Riviera in the early hours of the morning of 15 August, at approximately 0500 hours. A landing to the west of the Rhône seemed unlikely, as the earliest it could possibly take place there would be after sunrise.

An air raid was carried out by the enemy against the city centre of Marseille at 2230 hours, and it was reported shortly thereafter that paratroopers had descended on the submarine pens and the southern parts of the city. This led the headquarters of the Nineteenth Army to believe that a seaborne landing at Marseille was imminent. However, it emerged an hour later that this parachute jump had been a diversionary manoeuvre. The paratroopers were dummies.

Luftwaffe radar units picked up the convoy at 2320 hours and monitored it throughout the night so that its movements could be followed precisely. However, it remained unclear from the reports that had arrived by 0300 hours on 15 August where exactly the enemy would land. The hostile naval units had been spotted in an area that extended from the seas south of Marseille to those south of Cannes. It was at about that time that the commander of the fighter units of the Second Air Fleet reported: '100–200 machines belonging to the US 47th Bombardment Group took off in southern Italy at 0002. These aircraft, which will be towing troop-carrying gliders, are capable of reaching the French Mediterranean coast within four hours after taking off!'

At 0455 hours, the LXII Reserve Corps reported from Draguignan: 'Large formations of aircraft above our combat zone.' Another report arrived from the reserve corps just under half an hour later: 'Enemy paratroopers four kilometres south of Draguignan. Aircraft approaching in multiple waves. Mobile detachment sent to conduct reconnaissance south of Draguignan!'

By 0800 hours, based on the reports that had arrived from all branches of the Wehrmacht, it had become clear to those at the headquarters of the Nineteenth Army that the enemy was carrying out an airborne landing near Draguignan and Le Muy and a seaborne one between Saint-Raphaël and the Îles d'Hyères. It seemed from the locations of the naval units that had been spotted that the enemy was focusing his efforts in the Gulf of Fréjus and the coastal sector between Cavalaire and the Bay of Saint-Tropez. The number of ships suggested to the German military leadership that there would be approximately four enemy divisions.

The airborne landing near Draguignan and Le Muy had taken the German forces by surprise. In order to deal with this dangerous enemy, the Nineteenth Army amassed all immediately available reserves and assigned them to Battle Group Schwerin, which had just been established in Aix under the command of Lieutenant-General Richard von Schwerin. There were two temporarily motorised infantry battalions, two anti-tank companies, one motorised assault company, and one horse-drawn artillery battalion. Two further infantry battalions from the fortress area of Marseille were also to be allocated to the battle group. This formation would immediately set off for Brignoles, 60 kilometres east of Aix, where it would be joined by the two additional infantry battalions. It would then advance through Le Luc and smash the enemy forces that had landed in the vicinity of Draguignan and Le Muy. The 69th Flak Regiment also moved off for Brignoles so that it could assume responsibility for protecting the battle group from air strikes.

Our railway artillery on the east bank of the Rhône was unable to be brought forward to provide support for the battle group, as the railway line between Aix and Brignoles had been destroyed. Air support could not be counted on either. When requested for assistance, the commander of the fighter units of the Second Air Fleet informed the headquarters of the Nineteenth Army that he would be unable to do anything before the evening of 15 August. Meanwhile, no reports had been received by 0800 hours as to the location of the 11th Panzer Division.

Throughout the morning, the enemy constantly flew more forces into the jump-off area near Draguignan and Le Muy, and he also continued, almost undisturbed, to land troops on the coast between Cavalaire and Fréjus. Even tanks were beginning to arrive, and it was becoming clear that the points of main effort for the enemy along the coast were the Bays of Saint-Tropez and Saint-Raphaël. While all this was taking place, the Nineteenth Army sought desperately to bring reserves from the west bank of the Rhône to the east.

By shortly after midday, the nonstop bombing conducted by enemy aircraft had resulted in the destruction or weakening of all bridges across the river between Arles and Lyon. There remained no road bridges whose condition would allow the transportation of heavy equipment across the river.

The pontoon bridge across the Rhône at Avignon had also been bombed. Although the Nineteenth Army had at its disposal the resources necessary for the building of a new pontoon bridge, it decided not to go ahead with such a construction, for there was little doubt that a new bridge would be targeted and destroyed in an air strike almost the moment it was built. It seemed better to the headquarters of the Nineteenth Army to build ferries and to accept the inevitable delays that would result from their use.

The situation was particularly frustrating given the slow approach of the 11th Panzer Division, which was the only real combat-effective formation. By noon on 15 August, just one battalion of the 110th Panzer Grenadier Regiment and one panzer pioneer company had made it across the river. Otherwise, the leading elements of the panzer division were at that time near Pont-Saint-Esprit, located on the Rhône at a point 50 kilometres north of Avignon, and were unable to cross the river.[2] The 61st Panzer Reconnaissance Battalion and the 111th Panzer Grenadier Regiment were stuck in an area 40 kilometres to the north-west of Montpellier due to the destruction of a tunnel by the Maquis. In the

---

2   Elements of the I and II Battalions of the 15th Panzer Regiment, the 277th Army Flak Battalion, elements of the 209th Panzer Pioneer Battalion, and the 61st Anti-Tank Battalion.

meantime, there existed no signal communication whatsoever with the elements of the panzer division that had remained in the assembly area.

The panzer division dispatched reconnaissance units to examine the bridge sites. Based on the information that was gathered, the divisional headquarters concluded that it might be possible, with the full commitment of all available pioneer units, for the road bridge across the Rhône at Tarascon to be repaired overnight to such an extent that it would be capable of being used by medium vehicles.

By the evening of what had been a gloriously sunny 15 August, the situation at the beachhead was reported as having developed as follows: 'The enemy forces that landed in the coastal sector between Cavalaire and Saint-Raphaël, consisting of elements of several American divisions, have established a large beachhead and are advancing northwards from there in the direction of Le Luc and Draguignan. They are seeking to unite with the airborne troops and to push their way out of the hilly moorland to the north and north-east. The strength of the enemy forces that have landed from the air amount to that of a division.'

The measures that had been taken by the Nineteenth Army to bring about the destruction of the hostile airborne forces were unable to be carried out with the desired strength, as the destruction of the crossings over the Rhône meant that reinforcements could not be brought from the west bank of the river to the east. The hastily assembled forces already on the east bank consisted only of infantry units, and these were no match for the overwhelming materiel superiority of the enemy. Drawing on forces from the fortress areas of Marseille and Toulon was not an option, for this course of action had been forbidden by the Führer. Even so, the headquarters of the Nineteenth Army did not believe that it could accept the proposal of the commander of the 242nd Infantry Division, to whom it had entrusted the conduct of the attack against the enemy forces that had landed from the air. Specifically, Lieutenant-General Johannes Baeßler had recommended that no attack be carried out against the enemy airborne forces near Le Muy and Draguignan, where the LXII Reserve Corps had been encircled, and that a defensive line be established instead. In view of the weakness of our units, he feared that an attack would be lacking in penetrative power. In contrast, the army headquarters held the opinion that the valley near Fréjus, where much fighting was still taking place, could not simply be abandoned, for this would immediately give the enemy complete freedom of movement in the vicinity of Draguignan and Le Muy. The Nineteenth Army therefore upheld the order it had issued to Lieutenant-General von Schwerin to attack the enemy at dawn on 16 August and to re-establish contact with the 148th Reserve Division and LXII Reserve Corps in Draguignan. Flak and anti-tank units were to be assigned responsibility for providing cover against enemy forces in the moorland, while the inland defensive front at Toulon was to be held.

The attack that was launched against the enemy airborne forces by Battle Group Schwerin at daybreak on 16 August gained some ground to begin with. Later that morning, however, the battle group was opposed by waves of enemy air strikes, and new airborne landings to its rear meant that it ended up being partially cut off. It did not help that no more than one infantry battalion and one artillery battalion had been able to be assembled by the battle group on the night of 15/16 August for the attack the following morning. The remaining units of the battle group had been scattered on their approach march by continuous low-level air strikes, and the reassembly of those units during the night required a lot of time. Inadequate signal communications, firefights further inland with FFI units, and shortages of heavy – and particularly armour-piercing – weaponry confronted Battle Group Schwerin and the 242nd Infantry Division with an impossible task, especially given the ever-growing strength of the enemy. Nevertheless, by exerting all the energy at our disposal, which included the immediate commitment of any unit that arrived at the front, there was success on this day in preventing an enemy breakthrough in the direction of Brignoles.

By the evening of 16 August, the Nineteenth Army was compelled to abandon the idea that it could achieve any meaningful success against the enemy forces that had landed, especially given that the day had gone by without the desired reinforcements being able to be brought across the Rhône. The LXXXV Army Corps had managed to put vehicle ferries into operation at Arles (south of Tarascon) and Vallabrègues (north of Tarascon) at daybreak on 16 August and had commenced

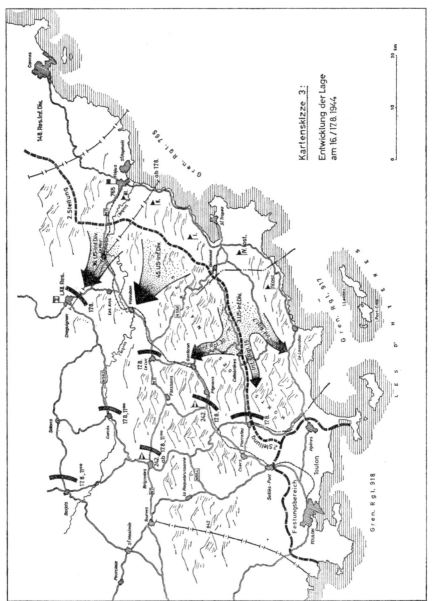

Map 3: Development of the situation on 16/17 August 1944

the transportation of the 305th Grenadier Regiment (of Battle Group Schwerin) across the river. However, the few available crossing points resulted in frequent disagreements between various units as to who should receive priority, and this required the headquarters of the Nineteenth Army to repeatedly intervene. The establishment of direct signal communications with the crossing points and bridge sites proved to be necessary so that the Nineteenth Army had at any time a clear picture as to which units had made the crossing of the river and which ones were yet to do so.

The 11th Panzer Division energetically continued its reconnaissance of bridge sites on 16 August. The reports produced from this activity revealed that the bridge in Ardèche (north of Pont-Saint-Esprit) and that in Roquemaure (south of Orange) would be capable of being used by vehicles and equipment of up to 8 tonnes. Based on this intelligence, it was decided by the divisional headquarters that its units would immediately set off in two march groups and that, with the 111th Panzer Grenadier Regiment in the lead, they would reach the designated assembly area, approximately 20 kilometres west of Aix-en-Provence, in the vicinity of Saint-Martin-de-Crau, Miramas, Lambesc, and Mallemort.

After it had become apparent throughout the course of the day of 16 August that the enemy, to begin with, intended to advance neither on Marseille nor on the area to its west, the Nineteenth Army took the decision to pull the 933rd Grenadier Regiment out of coastal defence at Marseille and the replacement training battalion of the 244th Infantry Division out of the coastal front at Toulon, and to allocate them to the 242nd Infantry Division, which had been given the task of occupying and holding the line of resistance between Pierrefeu and Le Luc. Because contact had been lost with the LXII Reserve Corps, with the last radio messages on 16 August reporting that its command post had been surrounded, the Nineteenth Army decided that the LXXXV Army Corps was to assume responsibility for the 242nd Infantry Division and Battle Group Schwerin. The main objective of the army corps would be to prevent any hostile advance from achieving a breakthrough in the direction of Aix, at least until the 11th Panzer Division had arrived there.

Given the difficulties being encountered by the 11th Panzer Division in its attempts to cross the Rhône, it could be expected that the assembly of this formation on the east bank of the river would be delayed for several days. It would therefore be the task of the LXXXV Army Corps to conduct delaying action towards Aix.

At a conference held between the headquarters staff of the Nineteenth Army and that of the LXXXV Army Corps on 17 August, the corps commander expressed his doubts as to whether the rear position that had been designated by the Nineteenth Army would be able to be held by the 242nd Infantry Division and Battle Group Schwerin until the 11th Panzer Division arrived. He thought it more advisable that a position on either side of Aix-en-Provence be established immediately. The commander of the Nineteenth Army rejected this idea on the grounds that it would allow the enemy to approach the assembly area of the panzer division on the east bank of the river much too quickly.

CHAPTER 2

Retreat of the Nineteenth Army through the Rhône Valley

Commencement of the retreat, 18–21 August 1944

On 18 August, the Nineteenth Army was confronted with an entirely new operational challenge. If all efforts up to and including 17 August had been aimed towards making the enemy work hard for every centimetre of ground and gaining time for our forces to prepare a counter-attack, those afterwards, in accordance with the order that had arrived from the OKW on the morning of 18 August, would be focused on bringing the formations of Army Group G to the north in a swift retreat. This would enable Army Group G to avoid the threat of being cut off and, once it reached the area near Dijon, to re-establish contact with Army Group B.

The initial considerations of the headquarters of the Nineteenth Army revolved around the question as to at what pace the retreat would best be carried out. The enemy would apply great pressure in his advance from the south-east, but it had to be borne in mind that the distance to be covered by the IV Luftwaffe Field Corps in its movement from the Spanish frontier to the Rhône Valley would be considerable.

If a rapid retreat was to be carried out by the Nineteenth Army, its route would need to follow the valley of the Rhône and subsequently that of the Saône. This route had been the main supply line of the Nineteenth Army since the beginning of the occupation of southern France. The mountains on either side of the Rhône meant that a withdrawal on a wide front would be quite impossible.

A further problem that would need to be addressed was the orderly return of all administrative and supply personnel who had accumulated in southern France during the one and a half years of occupation there. Such personnel included customs officials at the border in the Pyrenees, railwaymen in Marseille and Toulon, auxiliary volunteers from Indochina in the vicinity of Toulouse, members of Organisation Todt, and the professor for special tasks in Marseille with his two secretaries. There were three times as many non-combatants as there were combat troops, and their transportation would mean the use of the roads and railways to an extent that would hinder the flow of supplies to the front. However, it was essential that they be brought back in a completely organised manner so that the chances of mass panic would be reduced.

It was estimated that it would take until 23 August for the last soldier and last administrative official to be able to cross the envisaged line of departure for the retreat, the R-Line south of Tarascon. The question was whether the weak forces of the LXXXV Army Corps, even if supported by the 11th Panzer Division, would be able to hold out long enough against the enemy assault which was directed towards the valley of the Rhône.

Furthermore, there existed the great danger that the enemy, after obtaining full freedom of movement in the Aix–Draguignan area, could set off along the Aix–Sisteron–Grenoble road at any moment with the idea of carrying out an encircling manoeuvre in pursuit. The reason why this was a possibility was that the LXII Reserve Corps, with the 148th Reserve Division, had been subordinated to Army Group C and would therefore be falling back not to the north-west but rather towards the French–Italian Alpine crossings. This would open the way for an advance by the enemy to the north.

The 157th Reserve Division was in the Grenoble–Briançon area. Even though its regimental group was stationed in and around Grenoble, the reserve division, whose primary task was the security of the Alpine crossings, would be incapable of arresting an enemy advance from the south for any meaningful period of time.

It was advantageous for the IV Luftwaffe Field Corps, which was to be pulled back along the road on the west bank of the Rhône, that the inhospitable Cévennes Mountains would offer good flank protection against surprise raids by FFI units. The terrain on the east bank of the river, however, was perfectly suited for the conduct of an encircling manoeuvre in pursuit by the enemy, who would have many opportunities to gain territory there.

Along the 200-kilometre stretch of the Rhône from Avignon to Lyon, the foothills of the Western Alps extended towards the river. Parts of those foothills reached as far as the river itself, while other parts lay a little further back. These ranges of hills – rising between 300 and 800 metres, wooded here and barren there, in some locations ending in steep and rocky sharp drops and in others descending gently into the valley – were divided into three by the main tributaries that flowed into the Rhône from the east – the Eygues at Orange, the Drôme at Livron, and the Isère at Valence – and the eastward bend in the Rhône at Lyon. Each of the three ranges of hills lay approximately 75 kilometres distant from the next. Following the course of the tributaries were several good roads that connected the Rhône Valley and, running through the mountains about 75 kilometres further to the east, the Marseille–Grenoble highway. Constant attention would therefore need to be paid to the maintenance of strong security to the east whilst the withdrawal to the north was carried out.

It was highly unlikely that the enemy would initially apply strong direct pressure in pursuit along the valley of the Rhône itself. The bottleneck of the river valley to the north of Avignon would only serve to multiply our own defensive strength.

On the morning of 19 August, the headquarters of the Nineteenth Army issued its orders for the conduct of the retreat to all the units of the Wehrmacht that had been placed under its command. It also issued instructions regarding the conduct of the defence of the fortresses of Marseille and Toulon.

By this time, the enemy formation that had been identified before the front of the Nineteenth Army was the US VI Corps, with the US 3rd, 36th, and 45th Infantry Divisions. Also present was a British parachute brigade.

It was our impression that the enemy would only commit covering forces in the direction of Toulon for the time being and that he would attempt to force a breakthrough to the north-east along the valley of the

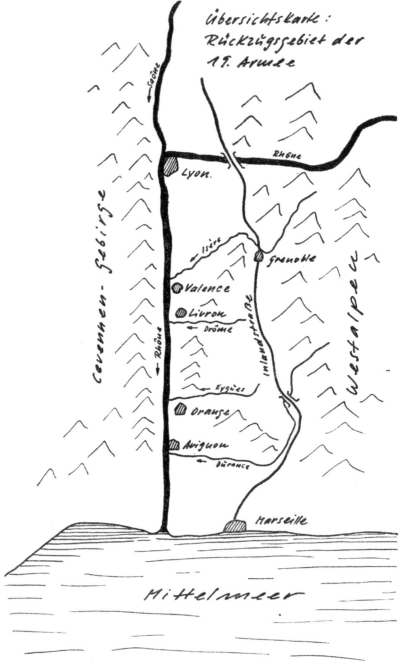

Diagram 1: Area of the retreat of the Nineteenth Army

Durance so that the German forces to the south of the river could be isolated. Nevertheless, there remained the possibility that strong hostile forces would advance from Draguignan towards Valence via Digne. It may have been the case that Digne had not yet been occupied by the enemy, but our lack of aerial reconnaissance meant that the headquarters of the Nineteenth Army could not be certain about the conduct of the enemy in this area.

Given the overwhelming strength of the enemy offensive, the troops of the Nineteenth Army were to be withdrawn to a new line of resistance connecting Saint-Zacharie, Pourcieux, Rians, and Saint-Paul-lès-Durance.

The LXXXV Army Corps had been entrusted with the conduct of battle to the east of the Rhône, and under its command were the following formations:

- On the right was the 244th Infantry Division, the bulk of which was stationed in Marseille. Two battalions were some distance from and were fighting their way back towards the inland defensive front at Marseille.
- In the centre stood three battalions of the 242nd Infantry Division. The remaining elements of the division, insofar as they had not been destroyed in the Allied landing, were located in Toulon.
- On the left was the 198th Infantry Division, initially with two battalions.

The IV Luftwaffe Field Corps had been assigned responsibility for all troops and all administrative and supply personnel – from all three branches of the Wehrmacht – who were falling back on the west bank of the Rhône. These forces would only be allowed to make the crossing to the east bank of the river if explicitly ordered to do so by the Nineteenth Army. Given that the retreat of the corps towards Lyon proceeded smoothly, with nothing more than a few negligible disturbances caused by the Maquis taking place, it will not be analysed in this book.

As far as possible, the senior quartermaster of the Nineteenth Army sought to arrange the transportation of all non-combat elements by rail.

The 11th Panzer Division, directly subordinated to the Nineteenth Army, was assembling with one battle group in the vicinity of Salon, another around Lambesc, and the 61st Panzer Reconnaissance Battalion in the vicinity of Cavaillon.

Even so, still standing on the west bank of the Rhône on the evening of 18 August were the bulk of the 15th Panzer Regiment (of which only eight Panther tanks had been brought across the river thus far), the 61st Anti-Tank Battalion, and the 119th Panzer Artillery Regiment (of which only the I Battalion had crossed the river). 12 trains with 40 Panther tanks were stranded to the west of Carcassonne due to damage to the railway line, and the destruction of the 8-tonne bridge at Roquemaure by aerial bombardment at 1800 hours meant that the 11th Panzer Division would no longer be able to transport replacement wheel parts across the river. Since the panzer division was most urgently needed on the east bank to ensure the security of the retreat, it was decided by the headquarters of the Nineteenth Army that all available ferries be placed at the disposal of the panzer division as a matter of priority. The elements of the panzer division that were stuck on trains were ordered to detrain and drive towards the river as quickly as possible.

The LXXXV Army Corps was given the task of conducting delaying actions in front of the R-Line so that the movement of German forces to that line could be carried out on the night of 21/22 August. After that, the R-Line was to be held until 23 August.

The 11th Panzer Division, in cooperation with the LXXXV Army Corps, was to do the following:

1. Move panzer combat units behind the front of and conduct operations in conjunction with the army corps.
2. Conduct reconnaissance towards the north-east.
3. Be ready to carry out attacks with limited objectives against enemy forces that were applying direct pressure in pursuit.
4. Reconnoitre and interdict all roads that led from the mountains to the valley of the Rhône. Particular attention was to be paid to the security of the area where the valley narrowed at Valence.
5. Annihilate enemy air landing units in the valley of the Rhône.

Carrying out these tasks would require of the panzer division that it split up its forces into battle groups. After so doing, the divisional leadership would mainly need to make decisions on the employment of three formations: the 119th Panzer Artillery Regiment (or at least those battalions, like the companies of the 15th Panzer Regiment, that had not yet been assigned to the battle groups of the 110th and 111th Panzer Grenadier Regiments), the 209th Panzer Pioneer Battalion, and the 61st Panzer Reconnaissance Battalion. The 277th Army Flak Battalion, although it belonged to the panzer division, had been assigned by the Nineteenth Army to the protection of the bridges in Lyon. Another important responsibility of the divisional leadership was the security of supplies to the widely dispersed battle groups, be they large or small. The flow of supplies was always guaranteed thanks to the full commitment of our supply services and despite the considerable number of broken-down vehicles.[3]

Weak elements of the battle group of the 110th Panzer Grenadier Regiment (Colonel Heinz Hax) went into action in the area to the east of Aix-en-Provence and Peyrolles-en-Provence on 20 August. The enemy tanks and infantry that were feeling their way forward in this area were repelled to begin with, but, given that our own units did not enjoy artillery support, they had to fall back towards Aix and the vicinity west of Peyrolles when the enemy renewed his attack that afternoon.

The 61st Panzer Reconnaissance Battalion thrust towards Apt and, by the late afternoon, had cleared the town of FFI units. After that, the battalion conducted reconnaissance along the Durance in the direction of Mirabeau, where the enemy had reportedly already crossed the river.

While there was a certain stabilisation of the front that day, the struggle continued to bring further forces across the Rhône. The staff pioneer officer at the headquarters of the Nineteenth Army wanted to dismantle the 60-tonne ferry at Vallabrègues on 21 August and put it into operation further to the north, at Pierrelatte, but the headquarters of the 11th Panzer Division objected to this. The bulk of the 61st Anti-Tank Battalion and the detrained elements at Carcassonne, including 28 Panther

3   Lieutenant-Colonel R. von Donath, 'Logistische Probleme beim Rückzug aus Süd-Frankreich', *Truppenpraxis*, vol. 8, no. 12 (December 1963).

tanks and approximately 500 motor vehicles, still stood on the west bank of the river. The chief of staff of Army Group G, Major-General Heinz von Gyldenfeldt, therefore decided that the ferry would remain where it was until the very last minute. There was a glimmer of hope that the replacement wheel parts belonging to the panzer division might still be able to be transported across the river, as the army staff pioneer officer believed that the railway bridge at Avignon might be repaired by midnight to such an extent that it would be suitable for use by light motor vehicles. Meanwhile, the divisional rearguard detachments in the vicinity of Toulouse were deprived of their vehicles by the headquarters of the local military administration, which meant that those detachments would have to march on foot if they were to reach the rest of the panzer division. The seven Panther tanks that could not be repaired in time and all armoured bridge-laying vehicles had to be blown up due to the lack of means of transportation for them.

It still lasted another three days, and thus 10 days in total after the movement order had been given, until the panzer division had ferried its last units across the Rhône at Pierrelatte and Montélimar. These included the panzer and panzer artillery units that had been ordered to detrain and drive to the river.

★ ★ ★

By 20 August, the headquarters of the US VI Corps no longer anticipated a German counter-attack to take place, for Allied aerial reconnaissance consistently produced reports about the commencement of a German retreat along both banks of the Rhône. As far as could be ascertained by the corps headquarters, the retreat was being covered on the right bank by the 11th Panzer Division and by two or three infantry divisions.

At 2045 hours, Task Force Butler was ordered by the US VI Corps to advance on Montélimar on the morning of 21 August and to block German forces that attempted to move through the town. This would be carried out in conjunction with the US 143rd Infantry Regiment, which was the regimental battle group that had already been sent on ahead by the US 36th Infantry Division and had been reinforced with a corps artillery battalion.

Combat in the vicinity of La Coucourde and Loriol, 22–30 August 1944

By 21 August, the columns of the Nineteenth Army were crawling to the north along both banks of the Rhône, but not always in an orderly manner. Lieutenant-General Johannes Baeßler, with the assistance of his headquarters staff, had his work cut out as the assigned traffic control commandant on the east bank of the river. Of the many men who made their way past him through the town of Pierrelatte, be they on foot or on horse-drawn or motorised vehicles, only a relatively small number belonged to combat units. Supply units and administrative personnel from all three branches of the Wehrmacht, as well as security, Organisation Todt, and auxiliary units – indeed, absolutely everything that could possibly have been amassed by what had been a static army for one and a half years – hurried through the town. They fully occupied the road leading to the town square and were repeatedly struck by low-flying enemy aircraft, leaving behind bloody trails and destroyed vehicles. Once it had become quiet, it was only with the greatest difficulty that this amassed group of men, animals, and materiel could get moving again.

At 1640 hours on 21 August, the 11th Panzer Division received the order from the Nineteenth Army to leave behind an armoured battle group on the front of the LXXXV Army Corps and to organise the rest of its forces into four battle groups, which were to immediately interdict the roads leading out of the mountains that lay to the east between Carpentras in the south and Valence in the north, with the objective of preventing the enemy from thrusting from the east into the route of retreat of the German forces. Combat-effective reconnaissance units were to drive as far to the east as possible.

Little was known of what the enemy was up to that day, especially as the Nineteenth Army still lacked any sort of aerial reconnaissance. At the front to the south, he applied only a small degree of direct pressure in pursuit. Ground reconnaissance units that had been sent into the mountains encountered resistance everywhere, but it could not be ascertained whether this resistance was being put up by FFI units or American ones. Only the 111th Panzer Grenadier Regiment, in an advance eastward from Carpentras, was able to clearly identify a group of American armoured reconnaissance cars with accompanying infantry. This group immediately fell back to the east when attacked by the panzer grenadier regiment.

The third general staff officer of the Nineteenth Army thought it likely that the US 36th Infantry Division had been committed in the direction of Digne. In the meantime, units of the US 3rd and 45th Infantry Divisions had already been detected before the front of the German LXXXV Army Corps.

In this situation, and at that time, the headquarters of the Nineteenth Army saw no reason to retreat more quickly than had originally been planned. Elements of the 11th Panzer Division would still be in the process of being brought across the Rhône at Vallabrègues on 23 August, so it was necessary for the LXXXV Army Corps to keep to the timetable for the withdrawal to the various new lines of resistance.

★ ★ ★

According to the reports that arrived at the headquarters of the US VI Corps on 21 August, the bulk of the 11th Panzer Division had by then crossed to the east bank of the Rhône and had intervened in the defensive fighting being conducted by German forces. The corps headquarters was thus compelled to put a stop to the offensive movements of the US 3rd and 45th Infantry Divisions.

The supply difficulties being experienced by the US 36th Infantry Division in its motorised advance towards Montélimar were considerable, but they were overcome by making use of the communications zones of the other two American infantry divisions. This even enabled the US 142nd Infantry Regiment, which was the second battle group of the US 36th Infantry Division, to arrive in Castellane by the evening of 21 August. The infantry division, which, after its arrival in the vicinity of Montélimar, assumed responsibility for all American forces that were committed there, received precise instructions from the US VI Corps regarding the establishment of a defensive line. The bulk of the forces of the infantry division were to carry out this task. It was obvious that the corps headquarters was already thinking about the execution of a destructive battle of encirclement against the German Nineteenth Army.

★ ★ ★

After being relieved by elements of the 338th Infantry Division, the 61st Panzer Reconnaissance Battalion was available for redeployment by the 11th Panzer Division in its efforts to carry out the order that had been issued to it by the Nineteenth Army. The bulk of the panzer reconnaissance battalion was committed to the area near Nyons, while the remaining units from the south-east and the west took up positions along the valley of the Drôme. On the morning of 23 August, the headquarters of the panzer division intended to position the reinforced 111th Panzer Grenadier Regiment in the vicinity of La Bégude, which lay to the east of Montélimar.

Troops of the 61st Panzer Reconnaissance Battalion came into contact with the enemy at Nyons on the morning of 22 August, although it was not clear whether the hostile forces belonged to the Americans or the FFI. After that, at 1400 hours, German columns to the north of Montélimar came under enemy infantry and mortar fire. This need not have come as too great a surprise. The Maquis had been highly active, and firefights had already broken out in the vicinity of Montélimar on 21 August. In addition, we were aware that the units of the French Resistance had received air deliveries of heavy weaponry from the Americans.

Three hours later, it had become evident that the enemy was carrying out an encircling manoeuvre in pursuit near and to the north of Montélimar. His anti-tank and artillery units had intervened in the fighting there in the meantime. At 1700 hours, the 61st Panzer Reconnaissance Battalion reported that it had taken prisoners from the US 36th Infantry Division at Puy-Saint-Martin, which lay 20 kilometres to the northeast of Montélimar.

At 1700 hours, the Nineteenth Army ordered the 11th Panzer Division to strike northwards through Montélimar in the direction of Loriol and to hurl back the enemy from the high ground he had occupied so that the road along the Rhône could be made clear for the retreat being conducted by the Nineteenth Army. For the execution of this task, the

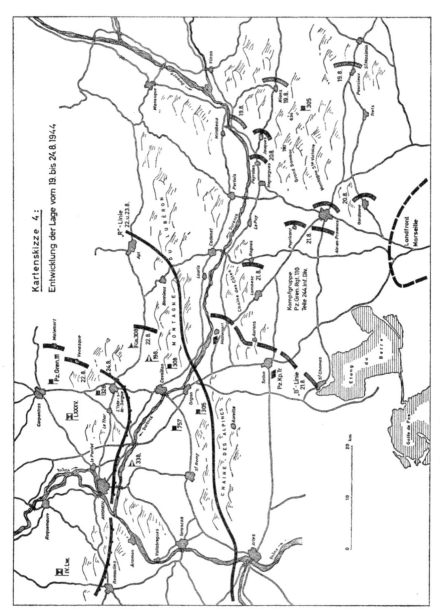

Map 4: Development of the situation, 19–24 August 1944

LXXXV Army Corps was to see to it that the 110th Panzer Grenadier Regiment (minus one battalion but reinforced with tanks), the 111th Panzer Grenadier Regiment, and the 61st Panzer Reconnaissance Battalion were relieved as quickly as possible.

★ ★ ★

When the commander of the US VI Corps arrived in the obstacle zone near Montélimar on the morning of 22 August, it was immediately obvious to him that the US 36th Infantry Division had been unable to establish the defensive line in accordance with the orders that had been issued. The corps artillery battalion was not yet in position, while the battle group of the US 143rd Infantry Regiment, instead of holding the line at Montélimar alongside Task Force Butler, had set off for Grenoble, as it had been reported that German forces were approaching from there. The battle group of the US 141st Infantry Regiment had received no orders whatsoever and was thus still bivouacked.

The US VI Corps ordered the US 36th Infantry Division to immediately bring back the US 143rd Infantry Regiment to Montélimar. The US 179th Infantry Regiment (of the US 45th Infantry Division) was to advance on Grenoble instead. Holding the defensive line to the north of Montélimar would be the responsibility of the US 36th Infantry Division, and it had to be borne in mind that it was quite possible that the Germans would attempt to drive from the east into the obstacle zone.

A German panzer officer, probably from the 61st Panzer Reconnaissance Battalion, was captured during the fighting at Puy-Saint-Martin. He had maps in his possession on which were marked the intended movements of the 11th Panzer Division.

★ ★ ★

The terrain in which the enemy had established his obstacle zone was particularly advantageous for him. Immediately to the north of Montélimar was the considerably broken massif of the Forêt de Marsanne, whose foothills stretched westwards to the Rhône and northwards to the Drôme.

The terrain to the north of Montélimar ascended gently to begin with, but, after a few kilometres, it rose abruptly into mountain ranges covered in woodlands. The mountain tops offered a good view of the entire Rhône Valley to the south, west, and north. It was rather like looking at a military map. Since the land between the mountain tops and the river was purely agricultural, it offered no possibility of concealment whatsoever. It was therefore the case that he who managed to seek cover in the woodlands on the mountains was the master of the valley of the Rhône between Montélimar and the Drôme.

Such terrain was disadvantageous for the conduct of an attack by the 11th Panzer Division, so the divisional headquarters requested that it be allocated a heavy field howitzer battalion. This request was rejected by the Nineteenth Army, as the battalion was required on the southern front. Instead, the panzer division received just a heavy flak battalion with two batteries. This meant that the attack, to which the panzer division would be committing the I Battalion of the 110th Panzer Grenadier Regiment (reinforced with elements of the 119th Replacement Training Battalion and 10 Panther tanks), would be lacking in adequate artillery support. Since the approach roads for the attack were totally congested, the headquarters of the panzer division requested that they be cleared for the motorised advance. The headquarters of the Nineteenth Army promised that this would be done. Nevertheless, the roads continued to be blocked throughout the night, which wreaked havoc with the timing for the approach of the panzer division and for the execution of the attack. This was not in any way the fault of the traffic control commandant, who had done his utmost to try to ensure the continued flow of the advancing panzer units.

Only on the late morning of 23 August did the attack get going at La Coucourde in the direction of the mountain range of the Forêt de Marsanne. It failed to reach its objective. The enemy had committed strong artillery units to the fighting, and our infantry forces were far too weak to be able to push the enemy back much further than slightly downhill on the outskirts of La Coucourde. The enemy remained where he was on the dominant hills to the east and fired at anything that moved along the road or across the terrain.

The reconnaissance foray being carried out by elements of the 61st Panzer Reconnaissance Battalion from Montélimar to the north-east ran into an American counter-attack. Reinforced with several tanks, the Americans hurled the weak forces of the German battalion back to their original line of departure.

Based on the intelligence that had been gathered on the enemy by the evening of 23 August, the headquarters of the Nineteenth Army concluded that the enemy would set up a defensive line at La Coucourde and that he would also most likely launch a strong attack towards La Coucourde from the vicinity of La Bégude. The Nineteenth Army therefore ordered the 11th Panzer Division, once the 63rd Air Regiment had arrived and had been placed under its command, to put reserve troops reinforced with panzer units on standby near Sauzet, which lay to the north-east of Montélimar. The LXXXV Army Corps was given the order to relieve all elements of the 11th Panzer Division still to be found in the Carpentras–Vaison–Nyons area and to see to it that they would be able to go into action at Montélimar.

After the failure of the attack that day, it was the intention of the headquarters of the panzer division to launch an assault during the night and seize the hills to the east of La Coucourde.

★ ★ ★

On 23 August, the US 36th Infantry Division reported to the US VI Corps that the positions to the north of Montélimar had been pushed further forward towards the road along the Rhône. In the late afternoon, the American attack on Montélimar was renewed, but it ran into and was brought to a halt by German defensive fire.

The German attack on Cléon that morning was repelled. Several tanks and anti-tank guns positioned to the north of Montélimar covered the road along the Rhône with fire. Two battalions belonging to the US 141st Infantry Regiment had gone into action, and so too had the corps artillery battalion and divisional artillery units.

The US 143rd Infantry Regiment had turned back from its advance on Grenoble and had arrived in the vicinity of Bourg-de-Péage. By that time, the headquarters of the US 36th Infantry Division was of the view that the forces that had thus far assembled near Marsanne would be strong enough to hold the defensive line, so it was decided that the

US 143rd Infantry Regiment would instead be committed to the narrow valley area of Valence.

Due to the reports of the presence of the 11th Panzer Division to the north of the Durance, the US VI Corps ordered the US 3rd Infantry Division to resume its advance. The German forces would thereby be pushed against the defensive line at Montélimar from the south.

★ ★ ★

Having been weakened during the day attack, the elements of the 11th Panzer Division achieved little more in the night attack other than the establishment of contact with the security forces that held the Livron–Loriol area. What was needed to drive the enemy out of the hills was massed artillery, but that was precisely what we did not have. As a result, there was no success during the night in getting into motion the columns that had accumulated in Montélimar. Enemy 15-centimetre guns concentrated their fire on the bridge site in Livron, and it was not long before the serpentine road leading through Loriol had become congested. When dawn broke on 24 August, any hope of moving our formations died away. The main road was cluttered with the wreckage of destroyed materiel, and all secondary roads along which we had conducted reconnaissance beforehand would no longer be safe to use, for the enemy was monitoring the entire area with artillery observation aircraft and directing his fire accordingly.

At 1030 hours, a radio message arrived at the headquarters of the Nineteenth Army from the headquarters of German Army Area Southern France, based in Lyon, which stated that Grenoble had been in the hands of the enemy since 22 August and that American tanks had already advanced to a point 40 kilometres to the south-east of Lyon. Strong FFI units were gathering in the vicinity of Lyon, an attack on which was expected to take place on 25 August.

Two hours later, at 1230 hours, Army Group G radioed the Nineteenth Army:

> The enemy is to the south-east of Paris with his southern wing advancing from Sens towards Troyes. Utmost acceleration of the withdrawal movement of the Nineteenth Army is necessary. The 11th Panzer Division shall maintain its role

as rearguard against enemy forces. Every battalion that the Nineteenth Army can bring as far as Dijon will be of the greatest value, for this will enable the Nineteenth Army to protect its flank there and to the north. The headquarters of Army Group G will be shifted to Dijon so that the establishment of flank protection can be properly organised.

Signed Blaskowitz

At 1400 hours, the Nineteenth Army issued the following order to the 11th Panzer Division:

1. The enemy holds the high ground to the northeast of Montélimar and thus interdicts the route of retreat to the north.
2. The 198th Infantry Division is being brought forward as quickly as possible for the conduct of the penetration through the narrow valley area to the north-east of Montélimar. The LXXXV Army Corps is assigning all available vehicles in the communications zone of Montélimar to one regiment of the 198th Infantry Division so that its troops can move with greater speed.
3. Corps Group Wietersheim, to be led by the commander of the 11th Panzer Division, is to be formed and made up of:
    ° 11th Panzer Division
    ° 198th Infantry Division
    ° 2nd Artillery Command
    ° 18th Flak Regiment
4. Starting from the line connecting the north-western outskirts of La Bégude and the town of Savasse, Corps Group Wietersheim shall advance rapidly through the high ground north-east of Montélimar to the Drôme between Grâne and Loriol. The intermediate terrain is to be cleared of enemy forces, and a defensive line is to be established to the east. The enemy troops in the area belong to a subordinate group of the US 36th Infantry Division. The more quickly action is taken, the greater the success will be.
5. The withdrawal movement of the LXXXV Army Corps will continue according to schedule. Forces belonging to the 11th Panzer Division will assume responsibility for the protection of the deep eastern flank.
6. From the morning of 25 August, the command post of the Nineteenth Army will be located in the area to the south-east of Montélimar.

Headquarters of the Nineteenth Army, Operations Group
8786/44, Top Secret

The Nineteenth Army requested air support for the attack on 25 August. Bombers and ground-attack aircraft were to strike Marsanne, which lay

15 kilometres to the north-east of Montélimar, by 1100 hours, and they were also, without any time limit, to target localities, troop movements, troop assemblies, and roads to the east of the line connecting Crest and Puy-Saint-Martin.

In making the decision to form Corps Group Wietersheim, the headquarters of the Nineteenth Army had in mind the idea that the 11th Panzer Division would have a particular interest in the success of the attack of the now subordinate 198th Infantry Division, and that the panzer division would therefore place at the disposal of the infantry division tanks or assault guns from its anti-tank battalion for the conduct of the attack. However, this idea took into consideration neither the absence of leadership coordination nor the inadequacy of the means of signal communication between the two divisions, and it ought to be added that the troops of those divisions were unfamiliar with one another. The headquarters of the 198th Infantry Division could well be forgiven for thinking that its troops were to be used as cannon fodder. Such thoughts would not help to lend momentum to the attack. Meanwhile, there was a dramatic revival of combat activity that afternoon near La Coucourde and Montboucher, where the I and III Battalions of the 63rd Air Regiment had gone into action. To the south of La Coucourde, enemy tanks, supported by heavy artillery fire, succeeded in pushing as far as the main road at a point 2 kilometres to the north-east of Montélimar. The Luftwaffe ground troops that were located there defended as best they could, but, unaccustomed as they were to infantry warfare, they suffered heavy casualties. The 11th Panzer Division therefore launched an attack at 1600 hours with the recently arrived II Battalion of the 111th Panzer Grenadier Regiment. This battalion was reinforced with 10 Panther tanks organised into two groups. The weaker group, with four Panther tanks, advanced to the north-east, while the main group proceeded along the through road that led to the north.

The attack very quickly ran into heavy enemy defensive fire and came to a standstill. It had to be hoped that the joint attack of the 11th Panzer Division and, to its right and initially advancing on Marsanne, the 198th Infantry Division on 25 August would shatter the enemy defensive line and enable German forces to push forward along the through road.

Depending on the development of the situation, the headquarters of the LXXXV Army Corps wanted to keep its formations close together so that any successful attack launched by the enemy would be incapable of driving a wedge between the German attack group and the army corps itself. It also wanted to negotiate the narrow stretch of the valley more quickly than planned. The first measure to be taken in this regard by the army corps was to bring forward a grenadier regiment so that it could be used to reinforce the attack.[4]

The evening report of the 11th Panzer Division to the Nineteenth Army clearly pointed out what a difficult battle was in store if the German troops were to extricate themselves from the encircling manoeuvre being conducted by the enemy. An enemy map that had fallen into German hands revealed that a hostile attack could be expected in the direction of Valence and that a new defensive line was intended to be established there:

11th Panzer Division

2100 hours
24 August 1944

To: Headquarters of the Nineteenth Army

Re: Daily report

The enemy has detected the effort being made by the 11th Panzer Division to force its way along the Montélimar–Valence road. While he remained quiet on the right wing of the panzer division in the vicinity of Nyons and La Bégude, he sought throughout the morning to take the dominant high ground to the north-east of Montélimar as well as the town itself by conducting repeated attacks against the II Battalion of the 110th Panzer Grenadier Regiment and against the ground troops of the Luftwaffe field battalion. The attacks against the II Battalion were repelled, partly in terrain with primeval forest and in close combat with cold steel. Aside from locations where minor penetrations of the front have taken place and against which counter-thrusts are still being carried out, the front line remains unchanged. Our own attacks to close the gap that has come into being in the combat zone of the Luftwaffe field battalion have ground to a halt due to heavy enemy defensive fire. The enemy succeeded there in pushing back our

---

4 The troops of the grenadier regiment were transported by motorbuses powered by wood gas. Many of these vehicles broke down on the way, which meant that the regimental group did not arrive in its entirety in time.

front to a point 2 kilometres to the north-east of the outskirts of the town of Montélimar. For now, the bulk of the Luftwaffe field battalion has been shattered because of the enemy attack.

Enemy tanks reached the road south of La Coucourde in the afternoon. Counter-measures are underway. The 61st Anti-Tank Battalion and the bulk of the 111th Panzer Grenadier Regiment are on the move in the vicinity of Montélimar.

It is intended that the 11th Panzer Division will advance to the north in the direction of Livron on 25 August. Immediately to its right will be the 198th Infantry Division, the first objective of which shall be Marsanne.

The success of the attack depends decisively on the arrival of the infantry, as our tanks cannot be employed to full effect in the rough terrain. On top of this, our tanks have already suffered much wear and tear after their drive of approximately 400 kilometres.

Enemy artillery fire was constant throughout the day. We have thus far only identified 15-centimetre guns being used by enemy artillery units, and they are being expertly directed by artillery observation aircraft. Hostile aerial activity is livelier than it has been the past few days, although no bombing raids have taken place.

★ ★ ★

The operations conducted by the US 36th Infantry Division on 25 August were significantly impacted by two problems. The first was that the divisional headquarters did not seem to be aware of what could be accomplished by a united formation, the consequence of which was that the division failed to commit all available forces for the establishment of a defensive line at La Coucourde. Instead, it pulled Task Force Butler out of the front and sent it to conduct reconnaissance in force in the direction of Loriol via Grâne. In addition, only elements of the recently returned US 143rd Infantry Regiment were positioned in the vicinity of Valence, while the rest of the regiment advanced on Crest.

The second problem, for which the divisional leadership cannot be held entirely responsible, was that it was deceived by false reports. It believed at first that its front line lay directly along the main road, but it was verified later that day that the Germans were there instead.

★ ★ ★

The attack led by Corps Group Wietersheim along the main road on 25 August failed to result in penetrative success. Due to the late arrival of the 198th Infantry Division, the attack only began to roll forward from 1100 hours and, on top of that, only in stages. Such a delayed and slow advance ought to have been avoided in view of the overwhelming materiel superiority of the enemy.

By 1330 hours, a group belonging to the 11th Panzer Division, consisting of elements of the 111th Panzer Grenadier Regiment reinforced with the 61st Anti-Tank Battalion, had attacked from the south-west and had succeeded in pushing the enemy back along the Montélimar–Marsanne road to a point just outside La Laupie. On the hills immediately to the east of La Coucourde, however, the enemy remained where he was and could therefore continue to keep the road under observed artillery fire. The five 8.8-centimetre flak batteries at the disposal of the panzer division were not enough to be able to force the enemy out of his mountain positions.

By the late afternoon, the 198th Infantry Division had launched its attack and had managed to push its front line forward so that it ran from La Bégude to Bonlieu.

It seemed in the early afternoon as if the main road was unobstructed once more, so the Nineteenth Army ordered the columns that had accumulated in the vicinity of Montélimar to move off to the north without delay. However, before most of the troops could get going, enemy tanks and infantry attacked from the area of La Coucourde in the late afternoon, overran the weak German security forces, and blocked the road as night fell.

When the non-stop heavy artillery fire on Livron resulted in the destruction of the road bridge there, all subsequent movements to the north by German forces had to be carried out across two fords to the west of the town.

The one success that could be reported by the headquarters of the 11th Panzer Division that day was the repelling of the attack of the US 143rd Infantry Regiment on Valence. With that, the danger that the enemy would establish a defensive line in the city was avoided for the time being.

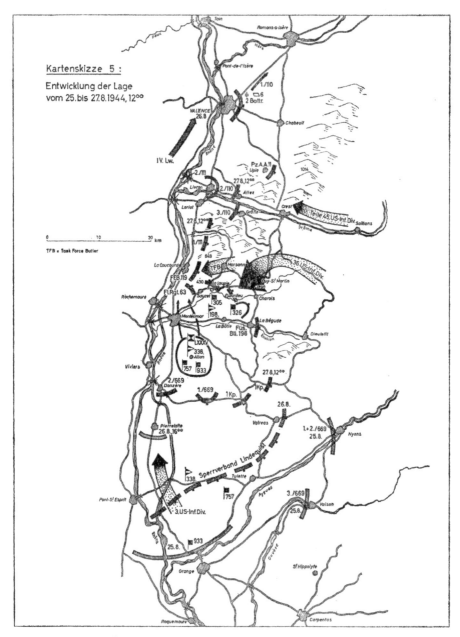

Map 5: Development of the situation, 25–27 August 1944

Contrary to the expectations of the headquarters of the LXXXV Army Corps, the enemy took no action on the southern front on 25 August and refrained from applying direct pressure in pursuit with massed armoured forces. The army corps therefore gave the order that the remaining elements of the 338th Infantry Division move as quickly as possible to the area north-east of Montélimar while the recently created Obstacle Construction Detachment Lindequist – composed of the 669th Army Pioneer Battalion (motorised), the III Battalion of the 338th Artillery Regiment, and the 2nd Company of the 338th Fusilier Battalion, reinforced with anti-aircraft guns – took over responsibility for providing cover to the south.

The attack of Corps Group Wietersheim on 25 August had made one thing clear: it was impossible for the headquarters of one division to manage the conduct of operations of two divisions. The headquarters of the 11th Panzer Division therefore requested of the Nineteenth Army late in the afternoon that it be allowed to relinquish control over the conduct of operations of the 198th Infantry Division so that it could fully devote itself to the tasks that it itself had been given by the Nineteenth Army.

The commander of the Nineteenth Army, General of Infantry Friedrich Wiese, approved this request during a conference with the commander of the LXXXV Army Corps, General of Infantry Baptist Knieß, held at the command post of the 11th Panzer Division. At 1815 hours, the army corps assumed responsibility for the 198th Infantry Division, and it also anticipated that the 338th Infantry Division would reach the area to the north-east of Montélimar during the night of 25/26 August.

At this conference, the 11th Panzer Division, as a matter of urgency, was given the task of eliminating at all costs the enemy forces that had penetrated the front at La Coucourde and of fighting its way along the main road after that. In addition, the panzer division was tasked with keeping open the bridges across the Isère at Pont-de-l'Isère and Romans-sur-Isère and with preventing the enemy from taking Loriol and Livron in an advance along the valley of the Drôme.

In a bitter night engagement involving tanks and infantry, the panzer division succeeded in pressing forward along the main road by 0400 hours and in hurling the enemy with his Sherman tanks back to Hill

262, which lay to the east of La Coucourde. From 0445 hours, the road was again under German control. Although enemy artillery continued to fire on the road at daybreak, it was believed at the headquarters of the panzer division that, if enough care were taken, the movements of the troops could be restarted.

The Nineteenth Army was prepared to accept considerable losses in terms of materiel provided the troops continued to move out of the encircled area. Only rapid movement would ensure the survival of the troops. Our most energetic officers were therefore assigned to the points of departure to oversee the dispatch, despite enemy artillery fire, of the German columns through the narrow valley.

The radio message that arrived at the headquarters of the Nineteenth Army from the headquarters of Army Group G on the morning of 25 August made it clear that combat-effective formations needed to be brought to Lyon as soon as possible. In accordance with this radio message, the Nineteenth Army ordered that every man and horse of the IV Luftwaffe Field Corps, with motorised forces in front, needed to make their way to the city without delay.

★ ★ ★

On 26 August, the headquarters of the US Seventh Army issued its order for the further conduct of battle. In so doing, it proceeded on the assumption that the German Nineteenth Army would go over to the defence in the vicinity of Lyon.

The US VI Corps was given the task of advancing on Lyon via Grenoble and Valence. Elements of the French First Army were to cross the Rhône at Avignon and take up the pursuit on the west bank of the river. Once Lyon had been captured, the US VI Corps was to proceed to the north along the Saône and establish contact with the US Third Army, while the French First Army was to push towards Besançon via Grenoble and Bourg.

The headquarters of the US VI Corps objected to this order, as it would cause the lines of attack of the Americans and the French to intersect and would thus bring about significant delays in the advance of the Allied forces. Contact with the Germans would be lost, making it highly unlikely that they would be caught before they reached the Belfort Gap.[5] Nevertheless, it took almost a week for the headquarters of the US Seventh Army to embrace the point of view of the headquarters of the US VI Corps. It was necessary for the US Seventh Army, in every decision it took, to show consideration for the stubborn and oversensitive commander of the French First Army, Army General Jean de Lattre de Tassigny, who was eventually convinced to agree to the change in the order when he was assured that the French I Corps could advance along the Swiss frontier beside the American forces.

While the US 36th Infantry Division had as its task the maintenance of the defensive line between La Coucourde and Loriol, the US 3rd Infantry Division was given the order to advance from the south towards Montélimar with all the strength at its disposal. In the meantime, the US 45th Infantry Division would continue the execution of the encircling manoeuvre in pursuit in the direction of Lyon.

★ ★ ★

The OKW telephoned the headquarters of the Nineteenth Army and insisted that the pace of its withdrawal had to be increased at all costs. The enemy had already reached Auxerre on 24 August, yet there were insufficient numbers of combat troops between Troyes, Dijon, and the Swiss frontier that would be capable of holding in check a sustained enemy assault in the direction of the Belfort Gap. Above all, the OKW emphasised that the 11th Panzer Division had to be brought to the north as quickly as possible.

Even if the headquarters of the Nineteenth Army had remained unaware of the overall situation as seen from the point of view of the OKW, all its efforts at that time still had to be focused on bringing as many troops as possible out of the ring of encirclement. An early capture of Lyon by the enemy could not be allowed to seal the fate of the Nineteenth Army once and for all.

After the 11th Panzer Division had reported at 0800 hours that the main road was again under German control and that the only way in

---

5   Translator's note: The Belfort Gap was an area of flat terrain between the Vosges and Jura Mountains, allowing an easier escape towards the German border.

which the enemy could exert his influence over it was with artillery fire, the Nineteenth Army issued its order for the escape from the encircled area. Excerpts from this order follow:

1. Only a small number of enemy guns are still able to fire on the Montélimar–Loriol road.
2. The escape of the 11th Panzer Division from the encircled area is underway. Following the 11th Panzer Division are the bridge column of the pioneer command of the Nineteenth Army, the staff echelon of the headquarters of the Nineteenth Army with the signal battalion, and the supply troops of the Nineteenth Army.
3. The LXXXV Army Corps is to relieve the forces of the 11th Panzer Division that are currently committed to the sector between La Coucourde and Loriol as soon as possible so that they can be made available for other tasks. The armoured group that is currently committed to the combat zone of the 198th Infantry Division will remain under the command of the LXXXV Army Corps.
4. Once the forces mentioned in paragraph 3 have escaped the encircled area, the army corps will withdraw its own forces to the north as quickly as possible. The obstacle line to be set up on 27 August will run from Donzère to Taulignan.
5. ....
6. It will be the task of the 11th Panzer Division to:
   (a) establish a defensive line between Grâne and Crest;
   (b) protect the east flank of the Nineteenth Army between Crest and Romans-sur-Isère;
   (c) conduct reconnaissance along the valley of the Isère; and
   (d) secure the mountainous terrain to the north-east of Tournon for the safe withdrawal of the LXXXV Army Corps.
7. ....
8. ....
9. The new command post of the Nineteenth Army from 27 August will be in Les Petits Robins, which lies 4 kilometres to the northwest of Livron.

Signed Wiese

If everything went according to plan, the headquarters of the Nineteenth Army could hope that the 11th Panzer Division would escape the ring of encirclement on 27 August, the 338th Infantry Division on 29 August, and the 198th Infantry Division on 1 September. None of the infantry forces of the LXXXV Army Corps could be expected to go into action in the vicinity of Lyon before 1 September.

The plans of the Nineteenth Army did not work out.

Difficulties arose as soon as our movements commenced. Shortly before 1000 hours, the first general staff officer of the 11th Panzer Division informed the headquarters of the Nineteenth Army over the telephone that the main road was blocked and that there could consequently be no thought of rapid movement. In response, the Nineteenth Army ordered the 11th Panzer Division to continue its drive without any regard for losses that might be incurred, for the failure of the enemy to launch an attack that day needed to be fully exploited. At both fords to the west of Livron, tractors were to be made ready to tow our vehicles across the Drôme.

Torrential rain started to fall at midnight, suddenly flooding the Drôme and making both fords to the west of Livron useless. It was not until noon on 27 August that the water had lowered to its previous level. That evening, two columns of the 11th Panzer Division stood to the south of the river and stretched all the way back to La Coucourde. The forces in those columns comprised the following:

- 25 Panther tanks
- 111th Panzer Grenadier Regiment
- 4th Company of the 61st Panzer Reconnaissance Battalion (with an experimental company)
- 119th Panzer Artillery Regiment (without the I Battalion)
- 209th Panzer Pioneer Battalion
- elements of the maintenance company of the 15th Panzer Regiment
- half of the 89th Panzer Signal Battalion
- command echelon of the 61st Divisional Signal Command
- one maintenance company
- one medical company
- 119th Replacement Training Battalion
- elements of administrative units

To bring these forces across the fords would take 12 hours, and that was not taking into consideration any influence that would be exerted by the enemy. Indeed, he had been attacking the 61st Panzer Reconnaissance

Battalion in the valley of the Drôme since the early morning and succeeded in pushing it out of Grâne. At La Coucourde, the 111th Panzer Grenadier Regiment came under such powerful attack that the headquarters of the 11th Panzer Division had to report to the headquarters of the Nineteenth Army at 1315 hours that, if the circumstances remained the same, it could be expected that the main road would once more be blocked by the enemy during the night. It was not yet known whether the panzer grenadier regiment could be relieved by elements of the 338th Infantry Division. Fortunately, the panzer grenadier regiment managed to put six hostile tanks out of action and thereby compelled the enemy to pause his assault until the evening.

In the south, the US 3rd Infantry Division launched an attack and lunged with its armoured spearheads and accompanying infantry as far as the command post of the LXXXV Army Corps in Allan. Only through the full commitment of all personnel of the headquarters of the army corps could a state of panic be avoided.

It was clear to those at the headquarters of the Nineteenth Army on the evening of 27 August that, aside from the losses in terms of men and materiel that had already been incurred, the extraction of German forces from the encircled area would come at the cost of most of their heavy weapons, especially those belonging to the infantry divisions.

The LXXXV Army Corps received the order from the Nineteenth Army to move out of the encircled area on the night of 27/28 August. The 338th Infantry Division was to be the first formation of the army corps to set off, after which the 198th Infantry Division, currently holding the wing of the army corps in the vicinity of Marsanne, was to disengage and follow the 338th to the north. Obstacle Construction Detachment Lindequist, reinforced with anti-aircraft guns, would serve in the role of rearguard near Montélimar.

The 11th Panzer Division, while continuing to carry out the tasks it had already been assigned, would assume responsibility for the protection of the flank of the LXXXV Army Corps against enemy forces that were advancing from the narrow valley area near Crest. Furthermore, the panzer division was to keep some of its tanks in La Coucourde, which had become a critical point for the conduct of operations.

By the morning of 28 August, the 933rd Grenadier Regiment had relieved the 111th Panzer Grenadier Regiment and was attempting to hurl the enemy down from the hills to the east of La Coucourde. Such efforts were in vain.

At noon, the enemy launched an attack on a wide front between Loriol and Upie, the latter being a village lying to the north-east of Loriol. The point of main effort of this attack was placed in the valley of the Drôme. In view of the small number of forces that the 11th Panzer Division had at its disposal to resist the enemy – and given that the heavy field howitzer battalion of the panzer artillery regiment had expended its ammunition and could expect no more to be supplied by the Nineteenth Army – it was feared that the enemy might finally seal the pocket along the Drôme on the night of 28/29 August.

Although the order for the evacuation of the encircled area was given over the telephone to the first general staff officer of the LXXXV Army Corps by the headquarters of the Nineteenth Army, there were doubts as to whether it was properly received due to the poor state of signal communications. To ensure that the order was indeed understood and put into action, General of Infantry Friedrich Wiese (commander of the Nineteenth Army) and Major-General Walter Botsch (chief of staff of the Nineteenth Army) informed Major Hiltrop of the situation and of the task to be carried out by the army corps, and, at 1720 hours, sent him to personally deliver the following order to General of Infantry Baptist Knieß (the commander of the army corps):

> The LXXXV Army Corps is ordered to withdraw any forces still to the south of the Drôme northwards across the river as quickly as possible because the 11th Panzer Division, from the morning of 29 August, will no longer be available to serve in the role of rearguard or to provide cover on the deep east flank.

The way in which the mission undertaken by Major Hiltrop unfolded is best described in the original report and is therefore quoted here:

> *1730 hours*
>
> The fourth general staff officer of the Nineteenth Army, Major Hiltrop, set off on his motorcycle to find the command post of the LXXXV Army Corps so that

he could deliver the order, ascertain the details of the situation, and determine the grounds for the delayed advance of the 338th Infantry Division.

1800 hours

The fourth general staff officer of the Nineteenth Army met with the first general staff officer of the LXXXV Army Corps at the new corps command post, 2 kilometres to the north-west of Livron. The first general staff officer had just come back from Command Post Knieß, north of Montélimar, with the latest details of the situation, and the fourth general staff officer immediately dispatched the liaison officer who had also just arrived there to the headquarters of the Nineteenth Army with those details.

1840 hours

On the Montélimar–Loriol road, the fourth general staff officer of the Nineteenth Army handed the commander of the LXXXV Army Corps the order from the commander of the Nineteenth Army. The fourth general staff officer emphasised that combat-effective elements of both divisions had to be brought across the Drôme this evening with all the means at our disposal.

The corps commander replied by saying that everything was already being done and that the divisional commanders felt the need for great haste. He did not know what further action could be taken. The order from the Nineteenth Army had already been given over the telephone by Major Becker, and the divisional commanders had already been informed of the overall situation. He and his chief of staff pointed out that the main road was completely congested and that the fixed fire of enemy mortars and multiple rocket launchers at Les Rey, a small village near La Coucourde, caused further difficulties. They insisted that there could be no thought of vehicles setting off tonight, particularly if, as was to be reasonably expected, enemy tanks were to occupy the main road.

The fourth general staff officer of the Nineteenth Army suggested that two tanks could be used to clear the road and that all units that did not need to use that road (i.e. infantry units) could continue their northward movement to the west of the railway line. The road from the southern outskirts of La Coucourde to the southern outskirts of Loriol was currently cluttered with the wrecks of motorised vehicles, horse-drawn vehicles, ambulances, and tracked vehicles. Everything therefore had to be brought to the north immediately in a manner that avoided the main road, something that might just be possible given that there was no guarantee from the morning of 29 August that the narrow valley between La Coucourde and Loriol could be kept clear of enemy forces. In fact, the enemy had already been trying since noon to push towards Loriol and Livron from the east, south-east, and south.

1915 hours

The commander and the chief of staff of the LXXXV Army Corps and the fourth general staff officer of the Nineteenth Army set off for the new command post. They had to stop at the northern outskirts of Les Rey, for the bridge there had again come under well-aimed enemy fire.

2000 hours

The chief of staff of the LXXXV Army Corps and the fourth general staff officer of the Nineteenth Army continued on their way to the new Command Post Knieß while the commander of the army corps followed later along the road, made known to him by the fourth general staff officer, which ran from Saulce to Gacavel, the western of the two fords.

2100 hours

The fourth general staff officer of the Nineteenth Army reminded the commander of the army corps as well as the corps flak commander, Colonel [Georg] Tyroller, of the order of the commander of the Nineteenth Army and recommended that the rapid northward movement of both divisions be carried out by exploiting all available fords and bridges and by obtaining the protection of some of the corps flak units which were currently being usefully employed in the role of artillery between Livron and Les Petits Robins. He also again suggested that tanks be used to clear the road and that the units to the south of the Drôme be pulled out quickly without regard for any losses that might be sustained.

The headquarters of the army corps has been deprived of its most effective means of issuing orders (radio stations, telephone communications, and orderly officers), which means that its most essential headquarters staff must take direct control of the movements of the troops. The chief of staff of the army corps is seeing to the concentration of the units to the north of the Drôme so that they can be committed to the protection of the east flank.

2215 hours

The fourth general staff officer returned to the headquarters of the Nineteenth Army and informed the army commander of the situation in the combat zone of the LXXXV Army Corps, conveyed to him the assessment of the situation of the corps commander, and, in accordance with the orders he had been given himself, provided his own appraisal of the situation: 'The LXXXV Army Corps does not appear to be in the position to be able to bring considerable elements of both divisions across the Drôme tonight. The 198th Infantry Division, engaged in battle to the north of Montélimar and constantly under attack from the south and east, is unable to disengage. A panic-stricken withdrawal would simply sweep up German units standing to the north of La Coucourde and would bring about the collapse of the entire front. The combat value of this infantry division is already limited given that the chief of staff of the army corps had to prevent an outbreak of panic when enemy tanks penetrated the front in the vicinity of Montélimar this afternoon.'

The fourth general staff officer continued: 'The army corps and the divisions under its command are so severely lacking in means whereby orders can be issued, especially in signal communications, that an organised retreat in accordance with the orders of the commander of the Nineteenth Army can no longer be guaranteed. Also, the commander of the army corps has requested that the 11th Panzer Division remain in the combat zone of his formation for at least two more days.'

At this point, the fourth general staff officer of the Nineteenth Army voiced his personal impressions: 'What is now most important from the point of view of the LXXXV Army Corps is to bring its formations across the Drôme in an orderly manner, to keep open the road from Montélimar to Loriol with all the means at its disposal, and to persuade the headquarters of the Nineteenth Army to leave the 11th Panzer Division where it is.'

When the army commander asked which elements of the divisions could still be withdrawn across the Drôme overnight, his fourth general staff officer responded: 'It is impossible to assess whether elements of the divisions can still be brought across the Drôme tonight or, if so, how strong those elements will be. The orders to the divisions could only be issued orally by the corps commander, and, at present, the conditions in the combat zones of the divisions and the assessments of the situation by the divisional commanders remain unknown to us.'

The fourth general staff officer was of the view that the corps commander would again have to be informed of the overall situation by the army commander as clearly as possible. It seemed to him, based on the slow progress of the 338th Infantry Division and the tentative movements of the troops, that the unit commanders had not fully grasped the urgency of the situation.

After a short discussion with the chief of staff of the Nineteenth Army, it was decided that a meeting would take place with the commander of the LXXXV Army Corps together with the commander of the 11th Panzer Division at the command post of the 110th Panzer Grenadier Regiment. Given that night had fallen and that the road from Loriol to Valence was occupied by two columns of troops (elements of the 198th Infantry Division and 11th Panzer Division), such a meeting could not be expected to be held before 0100 hours.

2255 hours

The fourth general staff officer again set off for Command Post Knieß, this time to take the corps commander to the location of the conference. Meanwhile, it was intended that the liaison officer of the LXXXV Army Corps bring a telephone connection unit and radio equipment to the command post so that signal communications with the headquarters of the army corps could be re-established and guaranteed throughout the night. However, the liaison officer had already left to deliver another urgent order to the corps headquarters, so Lieutenant Falkental, the chief of staff of the 1st Company of the 532nd Signal Battalion, was sent instead by the first general staff officer of the Nineteenth Army to Command Post Knieß with the telephone and radio equipment.

29 August 1944, 0125 hours

The conference at the command post of the 110th Panzer Grenadier Regiment was delayed by the fact that the regimental motorcycle messenger was late in picking up the corps commander and the army fourth general staff officer at the road junction 4 kilometres to the north of Livron. Once the conference commenced, General Knieß provided a brief overview of the situation:

1. Our grenadier troops are making their way through seemingly impenetrable mountainous terrain of the kind never before encountered by the general.
2. The 11th Panzer Division has been unable to secure the main road, for it too is limited in what it can do in the difficult terrain and must therefore remain close to the road or on smaller slopes. Meanwhile, the enemy has occupied the highest mountain peaks and is able to exert his influence on all German movements.
3. Only through the concentration of our artillery in one location were our grenadier troops able to take possession of some high ground of decisive importance. The result was the ability to deny the enemy any influence on the road at that location. An immediate counter-attack launched by the enemy soon hurled our severely weakened grenadier troops back to the road, and this was at the very moment the 198th Infantry Division was to pivot and commence its movement to the north. At the same time, traffic jams to the north of Montélimar were exacerbated due to the panic brought about by enemy armoured thrusts towards the town from the south and east.
4. None of the weapons at the disposal of the LXXXV Army Corps can counter the best American weaponry, especially the heavy mortars.
5. Supplies of ammunition are low.
6. Despite the tremendous performance of the 198th Infantry Division, our formations are almost fully depleted of their combat strength.
7. Hardly any noteworthy elements of the infantry division can be expected to cross the Drôme by daybreak, aside perhaps from some stragglers organised into companies.
8. In conclusion, very few units will be able to cross the river tonight. Even if the order manages to reach the units before dawn, which is doubtful due to the poor state of signal communications, it will only be a handful of infantry

units of low combat value, with neither ammunition nor artillery at their disposal, that might be able to make the crossing.

The commander of the 11th Panzer Division pointed out that the secondary road to the west of the railway line would be an excellent way for the troops to advance to the north.

The chief of staff of the Nineteenth Army said that the narrow stretch of the valley from L'Homme d'Armes to Le Logis Neuf would be decisive for the movement of the troops on the south bank of the Drôme. In this stretch, there would be few choices for advancing to the north other than along the main road, even though it was subjected to nonstop artillery, mortar, and armour fire by day and heavy harassing fire at night. The fire at night is highly accurate thanks to the practice gained by the enemy during the day. The possibility of evading this fire at Les Rey is of no substantial consequence because the bulk of our combat-effective troops are stuck further to the south.

In the view of the commander of the Nineteenth Army, it was important that new rearguard units be formed with the help of the panzer division on 29 August and that the Isère be reached with the greatest possible speed so that the German formations would not be forced into a decisive battle in the massif to the north of Tain by the enemy envelopment. Bearing this in mind, he added that there was only one question that needed to be discussed, and that was whether action be taken without the bulk of the infantry divisions so that at least a part of the Nineteenth Army could be withdrawn to its new position or whether the panzer division be ordered to remain a few hours longer in the Drôme sector, even if this meant that its strength be put at risk, so that the rest of the infantry forces could be safely brought across the river. He also pointed out that Regiment Hax (the 110th Panzer Grenadier Regiment) was too weak to be able to withstand any further thrusts executed by the enemy, especially if those thrusts were to receive strong artillery and air support.

The commander of the 11th Panzer Division said that, if necessary, his formation could hold the current position for one more day, but this would require the employment of its last reserves and would render it incapable of conducting any further mobile operations. Its Panther tanks would be unable to return, and Group Wilde, which was in action to the south of Loriol and had not yet been relieved, would no longer be able to cross to the north bank of the Drôme. The elements of the panzer division – including Group Wilde at Livron, Battle Group Thieme at Romans, and the flak battalion at Lyon – would have to take up positions of all-round defence until they were eventually destroyed. 'In my judgement,' said the divisional commander, 'that is the situation that would unfold and is therefore what I am making the headquarters of the Nineteenth Army aware of.'

When the commander of the Nineteenth Army asked the commander of the LXXXV Army Corps whether he had given the order for the breakthrough to the north to be carried out, the latter responded that he had not. The army commander pointed out that the order had been given twice, that it was of decisive importance that the 11th Panzer Division be released for action further to the north, and that the formations of the army corps be extracted from the pocket by fully exploiting any opportunities that arose by day or night. 'Since noon on 28 August,' responded the corps commander, 'the only way in which such an order can be carried out is if the divisions were to break through to the north in battle groups while leaving behind all vehicles and artillery pieces.'

The chief of staff of the Nineteenth Army proceeded to provide an overview of the overall situation. Specifically, he stated that the enemy had committed three groups of forces to the execution of his encircling manoeuvre in pursuit:

1. Relatively weak forces (one reinforced division) are pushing forward along the Drôme. The terrain is favourable for the enemy and less so for our troops, as it does not allow any freedom of movement whatsoever.
2. A stronger group (one new division reinforced with Free French units) is advancing towards Romans and Tain via Grenoble. This advance presents the Nineteenth Army with the same difficulties as those to the north of Montélimar, as the conditions presented by the terrain are similar.
3. An enemy group whose strength is not yet known is advancing past the southern end of Lake Geneva towards Lyon and perhaps immediately after that into the Belfort Gap.

When requested to give his perspective on this overall situation, the commander of the 11th Panzer Division simply responded: 'Either the panzer division will retreat behind the Isère today without regard for the infantry forces located on the south bank of the Drôme or, in accordance with orders, it will defend the route of retreat through the valley and die there with honour.'

The army commander decided that the panzer division would defend the western ford to the north of the Drôme until approximately 1200 hours, after which it was to withdraw initially to Valence and then behind the Isère. When asked for his opinion, the corps commander replied: 'If the panzer division cannot remain for another two days, I will be unable to bring anything of combat value out of the pocket.'

After a short discussion with his chief of staff, the army commander said: 'My decision is final, and I will have to accept the possibility that the combat-effective units of the LXXXV Army Corps will be encircled and will thus be unable to be employed in subsequent combat.'

0235 hours

The commander of the Nineteenth Army issued the following order: 'The LXXXV Army Corps will fight its way out of the pocket to the north with all the forces at its disposal. To facilitate this breakout, the 11th Panzer Division is to defend the north bank of the Drôme for as long as possible before 1200 hours on 29 August. No withdrawal shall be conducted by the panzer division before that time. Once the withdrawal commences, it will be carried out in conjunction with the army corps. The forces of the army corps are to be assembled along the Drôme and, under the protection of the panzer division, are to retreat rapidly through Valence to the north bank of the Isère. The headquarters of the army corps will assume responsibility for the defence of the city of Valence and all its installations from Naval District Southern France by 1200 hours on 29 August. Tain will be the location of the command post of the Nineteenth Army from 0800 hours on 29 August.'

Given that all signal communications with both divisions on the south bank of the Drôme had been lost and that the personnel at the disposal of the corps commander, aside from his general staff officers, amounted only to one orderly officer and one flak liaison officer, it was decided that the corps commander would attempt to convey the following order to the divisions by making use of the radio station of the headquarters of the Nineteenth Army: 'To the 198th Infantry Division: withdraw from the main road, cross the Drôme, and head for Valence.' He added that this order was to be passed on to Courbière, the location of the headquarters of the 338th Infantry Division, as well as to Lieutenant-Colonel Wilde, the commander of the 111th Panzer Grenadier Regiment.

In addition, the 11th Panzer Division immediately made two motorcycle messengers available to the headquarters of the LXXXV Army Corps, which did not have any scout cars at its disposal at that time. Everything possible was to be done by the army corps, even if at night, to ensure that the order was delivered to both divisional commanders.

The chief of staff of the Nineteenth Army reported the appraisal of the situation to Army Group G, informed Naval District Southern France of the situation and of the task assigned to General Knieß, and then saw to it that the order for 29 August was issued.

Over the course of the next few hours, the fourth general staff officer was to attempt to establish some form of telephone or radio connection with the German forces to the south of the Drôme. It was hoped that this would help the headquarters of the army corps in the transmission of orders.

The radio station unit of the Nineteenth Army had arrived at the headquarters of the LXXXV Army Corps in the meantime, which meant that the army corps was now able to issue orders itself. However, by 0800 hours, neither the 198th Infantry Division nor the 338th Infantry Division had acknowledged receipt of the order from the army corps.

★ ★ ★

During these dramatic hours at the command post of the 11th Panzer Division, the fighting continued to rage around the pocket.

When confronted with the overwhelming pressure applied by the enemy, the elements of the 110th Panzer Grenadier Regiment that were in action in the valley of the Drôme were compelled to fall back to Loriol, and it was there that an utterly chaotic battle unfolded at nightfall. The confusion that arose during the incessant shooting in the town resulted in the railway bridge across the river, which had been repaired for use by the infantry, being blown up ahead of schedule at 2100 hours. The elements of the 11th Panzer Division to the north of the river between Livron and Upie were attacked by approximately four enemy battalions reinforced with tanks and were only able to hold their positions with the absolute maximum of effort. The danger existed that the enemy would block the main road to the north of Livron, so the panzer division established a rear defensive position along the ranges of hills immediately to the east of the road with all the reserves at its disposal on 29 August. Given the battered state of both panzer grenadier regiments and the continued shortage of ammunition available to the panzer artillery regiment, it was unlikely that the panzer division would be able to defend this position for more than 24 hours if the enemy pressure were not to abate.

Despite the great superiority he enjoyed in terms of materiel, the enemy failed to seal the pocket on 29 August. With tremendous tenacity, the 338th Infantry Division, in conjunction with the remaining elements of the 11th Panzer Division, repelled all the attacks launched by the enemy, a sacrifice that enabled some of the infantry units of the 198th Infantry Division to make it to the north bank of the Drôme on the night of 29/30 August. However, the two groups assembled by the LXXXV Army Corps to the north of Valence on 31 August still amounted to desperately little.

Approximately 1,600 men belonging to the 198th Infantry Division and 1,100 to the 338th Infantry Division managed to evacuate the encircled area. In terms of heavy weaponry, 19 artillery pieces, 15 infantry guns and mortars, and three anti-tank guns were successfully brought across the

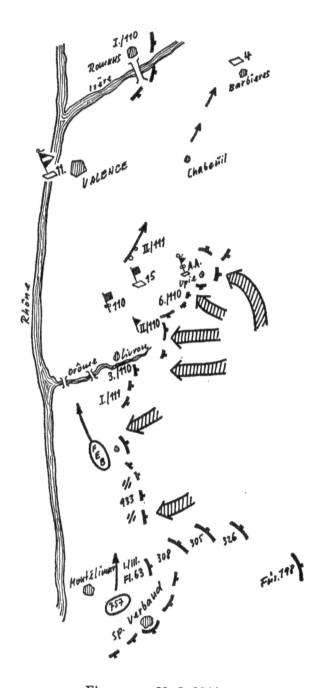

Einsatz am 29. 8. 1944

Diagram 2: Action on 29 August 1944

Drôme. The 11th Panzer Division lost not only 12 tanks, seven assault guns, and 14 heavy anti-tank guns, but also all the supply units of two artillery battalions. With such losses of assault guns and heavy anti-tank guns, the 61st Anti-Tank Battalion ceased to exist.

Meanwhile, the IV Luftwaffe Field Corps had received the order from the headquarters of the Nineteenth Army to send Battle Group Schwerin (composed of the headquarters of the 759th Grenadier Regiment, Battalion Marhanke, and the 116th and 163rd Reserve Grenadier Battalions) over the next bridges across the Rhône at Vienne and Givors so that it could prevent an advance by the enemy on Lyon by establishing a defensive line between Heyrieux and Pont-de-Chéruy.

★ ★ ★

The US VI Corps continued its advance from Montélimar on 30 August. While the US 157th Infantry Regiment proceeded through Aspres and Grenoble in order to establish contact with the US 45th Infantry Division, which was at that time approaching the Rhône from approximately 35 kilometres to the east of Lyon, the US 36th Infantry Division pushed further along the east bank of the river.

It was the task of the US 3rd Infantry Division to eliminate the German forces on the battlefield in the Montélimar–Loriol area. After that, it was to march northwards in the direction of Voiron.

★ ★ ★

With its forces stretched wide from Valence through Romans-sur-Isère to Beaurepaire, the 11th Panzer Division secured the route of retreat of the Nineteenth Army to Lyon. In the late afternoon, the headquarters of the panzer division received the order to shift some of its forces to the north bank of the Rhône between Meximieux and Miribel on the night of 30/31 August so that, from there, they could interdict the roads that led out of the mountains. Furthermore, the withdrawal of the rest of the panzer division would soon be necessary.

At a later stage, the panzer division would need to block the roads that led from the mountains to the area of Lons-le-Saunier, Arbois, and Dole. This task would require that the conduct of the enemy in the vicinity of Meximieux and Miribel be found out as soon as possible, and even that immediate reconnaissance in force be carried out in the direction of Arbois.

In response to this order, the headquarters of the panzer division requested permission to send a strong battle group to Dole at once so that the execution of an encircling manoeuvre in pursuit by the enemy in the direction of Belfort could be prevented. This request was rejected by the headquarters of the Nineteenth Army. Although the army headquarters recognised the danger posed by such a possible manoeuvre, it feared even more that the enemy might intend to thrust to the area north-east of Lyon with the objective of cutting off the route of retreat of the forces of the Nineteenth Army. Given that the analysis of our recent aerial reconnaissance soon revealed that the enemy was assembling strong forces at the crossings over the Rhône in Sault-Brénaz, and given also that the mountain roads in the direction of Belfort were reported as still being free of enemy forces, it was decided by the army headquarters that the bulk of the panzer division would be kept in the area to the north-east of Lyon and that its task would be to shatter the enemy attack that was expected to materialise from the narrow valley at Sault-Brénaz.

In accordance with the order it had been issued, the 11th Panzer Division arrived near Bourg-en-Bresse and Miribel by 31 August. From there, it was to meet the anticipated enemy attack between Meximieux and Ambérieu and secure the route of retreat of the Nineteenth Army.

For the movement of troops through Lyon, the headquarters of the Nineteenth Army issued a special order. The city had been a place of unrest throughout the period of its occupation. This meant that, until all elements of the Nineteenth Army had passed through and all bridges across the Rhône and Saône had been blown up, a firm hold on the city would have to be maintained so that any thoughts of an uprising while the retreat was underway would be quashed. After a briefing at the army headquarters given by the chief of staff of the 590th Regional Military Headquarters, the Nineteenth Army assigned the IV Luftwaffe Field Corps responsibility for the security of, evacuation from, and destruction of the bridges in the city. All forces that were defending the city outskirts or securing the city centre were at the same time placed under the command of the Luftwaffe field corps. A precise schedule was organised for the conduct of the retreat through the Lyon bridgehead, and it was envisaged that the last of its five phases would involve the final evacuation of the city and the destruction of the bridges on the night of 2/3 September.

★ ★ ★

The French Resistance fighters in Lyon were planning to initiate an uprising to liberate the city, but the idea was rejected by the headquarters of the US Seventh Army when it was asked about it. The only way in which such an uprising could take place was if it were agreed to by both the American and French armed forces. No agreement was reached, especially as the US 36th Infantry Division had already reached the eastern suburbs of Lyon on the morning of 31 August and the French II Corps stood immediately before the city on the west bank of the Rhône.

CHAPTER 3

Race to the Belfort Gap, 1–6 September 1944

The Nineteenth Army moved its headquarters to Chalon-sur-Saône on 1 September. In a conference with Colonel-General Johannes Blaskowitz that morning, General of Infantry Friedrich Wiese was given a broad overview of the situation in the West:

> The pivot of the US Third Army to the north-east at Troyes means that the danger of the lines of retreat of Army Group G being cut off by a massed advance of Anglo-American forces has subsided. However, the Nineteenth Army must be prepared for the possibility that the enemy might assemble a new group of Anglo-American forces at any moment and send it through Nancy and Belfort to surround the Belfort Gap. As far as can be ascertained at this stage, the formation of such a group of forces has not yet taken place.
>
> Army Group G has committed forces to the establishment of a security line which runs from Cahaumont to the Swiss frontier via Châtillon, Autun, Chalon-sur-Saône, Dole, Arbois, and Morez. The Nineteenth Army, moving from the south to the north, and the LXIV Army Corps, doing the same from the south-west to the north-east, are to withdraw behind this line.

The forces along the security line were composed of infantry units without heavy weaponry and were thus extremely weak.

In order to gain time for the conduct of the withdrawal of the LXIV Army Corps, the route of retreat of which was the longest, the headquarters of Army Group G ordered that the Nineteenth Army delay the advance of the enemy at the next three lines of resistance:

a) Mâcon–Bourg-en-Bresse
b) Tournus–Lons-le-Saunier
c) Dole Position.

★ ★ ★

Because of the constant relocation of the command posts of all formations during the conduct of the retreat, signal communications between the headquarters of the Nineteenth Army and that of the 11th Panzer Division were lost on the night of 31 August to 1 September. Contact with the IV Luftwaffe Field Corps and the LXXXV Army Corps was also unable to be maintained. The panzer division did not acknowledge receipt of any of the radio messages sent into the ether by the army headquarters, in which an update on the situation was requested. Only at 1415 hours on 1 September did the Nineteenth Army pick up a response from the panzer division, in which it was reported that the latter was engaged in heavy combat against enemy bridgeheads in the area to the south of Meximieux and against enemy forces at Châtillon and Priay that were constantly being reinforced with tanks, artillery, and multiple rocket launchers. Raids carried out by French Resistance fighters in the rear area were causing confusion in our assembly areas and disrupting our lines of movement. It was also ascertained that hostile tanks had appeared at Neuville, but, beyond that, the rest of the radio message could not be made out.

Since no radio contact had been established with the 11th Panzer Division by 2300 hours, the Nineteenth Army sent a liaison officer to deliver an order which stated that the panzer division was to remain in the Bourg–Meximieux area on 2 September, while other units under the command of Corps Dehner were to set up an obstacle line in the area to the southeast of Dole. Furthermore, the panzer division was to assume responsibility for the protection of the east flank of the Nineteenth Army on 4 September so that, with a particularly strong security detachment in the vicinity of Louhans, it could assemble for united action in the Gray–Dole–Besançon area. The panzer division was to remain on standby in this area and, in readiness to be sent in any direction, was to conduct reconnaissance accordingly. Any units there that would not be required to go into combat were to be withdrawn immediately.

The withdrawal from Lyon was conducted without any perceptible pressure being applied by the enemy. Bad weather meant little hostile aerial activity, which allowed the railway line to the north of the city to be used for the transportation of troops. Meanwhile, the situation in the combat zone of the 11th Panzer Division remained unknown until 1800 hours, at which time a radio message arrived with more precise information on the heavy fighting that had taken place on 1 September. It was clear from the report that the panzer division had almost annihilated the US 179th Infantry Regiment (of the US 45th Infantry Division) when the Americans had launched an attack from the area of Pont-d'Ain and Meximieux, and that this had rendered the enemy incapable of undertaking any major operation on 2 September.

In pursuance of the further conduct of operations as planned by the Nineteenth Army, the 11th Panzer Division had shifted a battle group made up of the 110th Panzer Grenadier Regiment, the II Battalion of the 129th Panzer Artillery Regiment, the 2nd Company of the 209th Panzer Pioneer Battalion, the 3rd Company of the 61st Anti-Tank Battalion, and four Panzer IV tanks to the area near Louhans. Meanwhile, a group consisting of the 111th Panzer Grenadier Regiment, the 61st Panzer Reconnaissance Battalion, the 209th Replacement Training Battalion, the III Battalion of the 119th Panzer Artillery Regiment, the 3rd Company of the 209th Panzer Pioneer Battalion, and eight Panther tanks remained in position in the vicinity of Bourg-en-Bresse.

In its report, the headquarters of the panzer division expressed the view that the enemy would set off northwards from Ambérieu-en-Bugey to continue the execution of an encircling manoeuvre in pursuit. This was confirmed at 2230 hours by the evaluation of our aerial reconnaissance, which reported that a column of more than 100 trucks accompanied by infantry, artillery, and armoured units was advancing from the town to the north.

★ ★ ★

On 3 September, the US Seventh Army agreed to the change that had been requested by the US VI Corps on 26 August regarding the order for the further conduct of operations. According to the new order that was now issued by the corps for the pursuit of the retreating forces of the German Nineteenth Army, the US 3rd Infantry Division was to advance as quickly as possible to the north-east in the direction of Lons-le-Saunier and Besançon, the US 36th Infantry Division was to push forward immediately to the left of the US 3rd Infantry Division, and the US 45th Infantry Division, after resolving the situation in the vicinity of Bourg, was to follow in the wake of the US 3rd Infantry Division.

At the request of Army General Lattre de Tassigny, the French I Corps was sent along the Swiss border in the direction of Belfort. The headquarters of the US VI Corps was not happy about this, as it was concerned that the freedom of movement of its forces would become increasingly limited as they drew closer to the Belfort Gap.

Supply difficulties arose for the Americans by the time they reached Lyon due to the fact that their supply lines extended all the way to the Mediterranean Sea. On 1 September, all depots of the US Seventh Army still lay to the south of the Durance. Only in the following days were there plans for a depot to be set up at Montélimar. This meant that, for the time being, the elements of the US 3rd Infantry Division committed to the pursuit of the German forces stood 250 kilometres to the north of their supply bases. On top of this, the US VI Corps was obliged to maintain the flow of supplies not only to its own but also to the French troops, for the latter were not adequately blessed with supply units. Despite this, the corps headquarters was convinced that the supplies being delivered by road, as well as by rail from Sisteron, would be sufficient for the advance into the Belfort Gap. It was also the view of the corps headquarters that it ought to be possible to intercept the German forces before they reached the Belfort Gap, especially since it seemed as if the German troops were in a rather disorganised state.

★ ★ ★

The overall situation caused the headquarters of the Nineteenth Army great concern. Placed under its command at 0600 hours was the LXIV Army Corps, which, although it was conducting a withdrawal, still lay almost 400 kilometres to the south-west. Also assigned to the Nineteenth Army and tasked with the provision of cover to the north-west, west, south-west, and south were Battle Group Brodowski, Battle Group Schmidt, and Corps Dehner. The commanders of these formations objected to being given this task due to the small numbers of troops at their disposal, and the army headquarters was forced to agree that almost any security or interdiction measures it undertook would in no way be enough to deal with the enemy if he were to concentrate his forces for a breakthrough at one location. The conduct of the withdrawal of the LXXXV Army Corps and the IV Luftwaffe Field Corps by the Nineteenth Army, although closely pursued by the enemy, took only a few days and proceeded smoothly, but it was a different story for the LXIV Army Corps, whose slowest elements could only march on foot and therefore could only be expected to reach Dijon in mid-September. Given the pressure that was bound to be applied by the enemy in the direction of the Belfort Gap, the army headquarters was confronted with the question as to whether it would be possible to await even those slowest elements without completely wearing out its remaining combat-effective units.

On 3 September, the enemy refrained from following the LXXXV Army Corps on the east bank of the Saône, which allowed the army corps to withdraw to the Doubs undisturbed. However, on the west bank of the Saône, the French 1st Armoured Division applied direct pressure in pursuit against and inflicted considerable losses on the rearguard units of the IV Luftwaffe Field Corps. A far more dangerous development that day, though, was the advance along the Swiss frontier of the enemy column whose presence had been reported by our aerial reconnaissance the previous evening. In the late afternoon, Corps Dehner reported that the enemy had pushed beyond Gex and that, because of this, uncertainty reigned regarding the fate of the German garrison in Morez and the Cossacks in Pontarlier. Consequently, at 2215 hours, the Nineteenth Army ordered the 11th Panzer Division to hastily send some of its forces into action to free the garrisons in Morez and Pontarlier and to block the main route of advance being used by the enemy for the execution of his encircling manoeuvre in pursuit.

The crisis at Pontarlier had begun. As General Wiese put it to his chief of staff: 'The moment of truth has come. Who will get there first? The 11th Panzer Division or the Americans?'

The Americans launched multiple attacks of battalion strength with armoured support against the 11th Panzer Division on 3 September. Although these attacks were repelled, the result was that the battle group of the 111th Panzer Grenadier Regiment still stood in the vicinity of

Bourg-en-Bresse that evening. The order to disengage from the enemy from 2100 hours was given. Leaving behind elements of the 61st Panzer Reconnaissance Battalion to serve as rearguard units, the battle group was to proceed through Louhans, Navilly, and Dole and assemble in the area to the north-west of Besançon. On the way, it encountered a unit of the 117th Cavalry Squadron (of the US VI Corps) at rest in Montrevel and totally annihilated it.

The battle group of the 110th Panzer Grenadier Regiment was already driving in the direction of Besançon. It could only be hoped by the headquarters of the Nineteenth Army that this battle group would reach the new zone of operations in time.

On 3 September, the only operational vehicles at the disposal of the battle-weary 15th Panzer Regiment were 12 Panther and four Panzer IV tanks, so the headquarters of the Nineteenth Army ordered that morning that the panzer regiment be reinforced with eight Panthers and two Panzer IVs from the 9th SS Panzer Division Hohenstaufen, which was at that time near Dijon. However, the army headquarters was compelled to cancel this order in the afternoon, as the IV Luftwaffe Field Corps was in urgent need of anti-tank defences. The SS non-commissioned officer in charge of the reinforcement group therefore had to be redirected to Chagny, which lay to the north-west of Chalon-sur-Saône. Unfortunately, the reinforcement group never arrived at its destination. In the chaos that reigned, the need to keep the headquarters of the 11th Panzer Division informed had been overlooked, and the result was that a lieutenant who came across the reinforcement group in the meantime took the decision to incorporate it into the panzer division.

In the early morning of 4 September, the leading elements of the battle group of the 110th Panzer Grenadier Regiment reached the area immediately to the west of Besançon. There existed no signal communications with the 11th Panzer Division and the battle group of the 111th Panzer Grenadier Regiment until after midday due to the shift in location of the divisional headquarters to Besançon. This meant that the headquarters of the Nineteenth Army had no knowledge as to whether the panzer division had managed to cross the Doubs. Even the precise locations of the units of the battle group of the 111th Panzer Grenadier Regiment remained unknown.

The 1022nd Security Battalion was sent by the Nineteenth Army from Besançon to reinforce the garrison in Pontarlier, but ended up being hopelessly tied up in combat with French Resistance groups at Valdahon, which lay 10 kilometres to the south-east of Besançon. Meanwhile, in the early afternoon, our aerial reconnaissance reported: 'Columns of tanks and trucks have been spotted a few kilometres to the south of Pontarlier, and additional columns of enemy troops are advancing in the direction of Lons-le-Saunier.'

The crisis was clearly reaching a climax. When contact was re-established with the 11th Panzer Division, the headquarters of the Nineteenth Army discovered that the battle group of the 110th Panzer Grenadier Regiment had been used to create an emergency cordon around Besançon on the east bank of the Doubs. It had been the intention of the Nineteenth Army that this battle group be employed 20 kilometres to the south of the city along a line connecting Mouchard, Salins-les-Bains, Levier, and Pontarlier, but this would no longer take place. American infantry units had already formed a small bridgehead across the Doubs at Avanne, 4 kilometres to the south-west of Besançon, at 1215 hours, and the panzer grenadier regiment had only just managed to establish a weak defensive line to keep the US 3rd Infantry Division at bay. This defensive line followed a series of forts and their garrisons and ran through Beure, La Vèze, Mamirolle, and Bouclans before bending sharply to the north and reaching the river at Champlive.

It would clearly be the intention of the enemy to make use of every opportunity to pivot to the north and press forward on either side of Besançon. In so doing, he would have to avoid the impassable massif that was Montagnes du Lomont.

To stabilise the front in the vicinity of Besançon, Army Group G ordered that the 159th Infantry Division, which had entered the Dijon area, be detached from the LXIV Army Corps and placed under the command of the Nineteenth Army. However, the plan of the army headquarters to send a regimental group of the infantry division as quickly as possible to Besançon and to place it at the disposal of Corps Dehner could not come to fruition, as the order from the army group, which was supposed to go via the army corps, did not reach the infantry division. Indeed, the infantry division had already marched off from the area west of Dijon in the direction of Remiremont.

On 4 September, contact with the enemy was lost in the combat zones of the IV Luftwaffe Field Corps and LXXXV Army Corps, which enabled the new positions on the north bank of the Doubs to be occupied without any great difficulty. However, in the Besançon sector, the enemy continued to apply considerable pressure. By the late afternoon, the road connecting Dole and Besançon was being subjected to enemy artillery fire at a point 4 kilometres to the west of Besançon. From the bridge site at Baume-les-Dames, which lay 12 kilometres to the north-east of Besançon, it was reported that enemy armoured reconnaissance units had appeared and that they were attempting to cross the Doubs there.

It was decided at the headquarters of the Nineteenth Army that no additional forces would be moved to the south bank of the Doubs. Instead, all available forces would interdict the valley through which the river ran or, alternatively, would swing back via Montbéliard and approach the Swiss frontier from the north to cut through what was presumed to be the main route of advance of the enemy. In this regard, the headquarters of Army Group G requested that, if possible, the left wing be pushed forward to Morteau, 20 kilometres to the north-east of Pontarlier.

The only formation available to the Nineteenth Army for the execution of these tasks was the 11th Panzer Division with the battle group of the 111th Panzer Grenadier Regiment, the leading elements of which had crossed the Doubs at Navilly at noon. The divisional headquarters took the decision to send the 61st Panzer Reconnaissance Battalion through L'Isle-sur-le-Doubs so that it could establish a defensive line between Doubs and Pont-de-Roide and, if possible, conduct reconnaissance to the south. As a security measure, the 277th Army Flak Battalion was dispatched to Montbéliard.

★ ★ ★

The US VI Corps, standing by with a northward-facing front on the morning of 5 September in readiness to conduct a thrust through Besançon in the direction of Vesoul, had positioned its forces as follows:

- The US 3rd Infantry Division stood on either side of Besançon with the US 7th Infantry Regiment holding the bridgehead at Avanne,

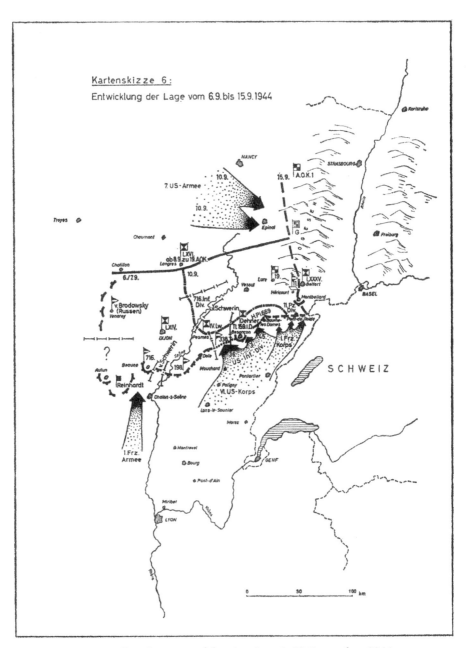

Map 6: Development of the situation, 6–15 September 1944

where, with the help of the FFI, an intact bridge had been taken, and with the US 30th Infantry Regiment encircling Besançon. From the high ground at Montfaucon, which lay immediately to the east of the city, the heavy weaponry of the US 30th Infantry Regiment dominated the arterial road leading to the east.

- The US 36th Infantry Division had assembled its forces in the Poligny–Arbois–Mouchard area.
- The US 45th Infantry Division stood at Baume-les-Dames.

It was the plan of the US VI Corps to strike across the Doubs on a wide front either side of Besançon and then, after reaching Vesoul, to pivot to the east and advance on Belfort via Lure. Meanwhile, the French I Corps was to proceed along the Doubs towards Belfort via Montbéliard.

★ ★ ★

At 0935 hours, the 11th Panzer Division sent the following report to the Nineteenth Army:

> All roads leading from west to east in the vicinity of Besançon are being subjected to heavy artillery fire. The enemy is attacking the positions of the 110th Panzer Grenadier Regiment to the south of Besançon with the point of main effort at Beure. At Baume-les-Dames, he has managed to cross the river, so the II Battalion of the 111th Panzer Grenadier Regiment has been sent into action there with four heavy anti-tank guns. All our tanks are still located to the west of Besançon.

Fighting raged throughout the day, and it was only after the panzer division had committed to battle not just its replacement training battalion but also any tanks that had arrived in its area that there was success in hurling the enemy back across the river. The strikes conducted by the Americans at Besançon were repelled, which meant that little territory was lost, although the bridgehead held by the US 3rd Infantry Division at Avanne was unable to be eliminated, for the forces required to do so were lacking.

To the right of the 11th Panzer Division was the 338th Infantry Division, which had managed to establish nothing more than a very thin line of security along the Doubs. This was because the infantry division had at its disposal only 100 men for every 4 kilometres of front line and only 16 guns in total for its entire 60-kilometre front.

Our aerial reconnaissance that evening reported that new large enemy formations were advancing towards Pontarlier and Salins-les-Bains. In full awareness of the fact that our forces would be too weak to be able to mount an effective defence against another encircling manoeuvre in pursuit, the headquarters of the Nineteenth Army contemplated the idea of pulling back the positions which were echeloned far to the south-west in the direction of Chalon-sur-Saône so that more forces could be made available.

The headquarters of Army Group G, having to deal with a number of restrictions placed on it from above, was unable to approve this plan. The army headquarters therefore prepared a memorandum in which the following was made clear:

1. The divisions at the disposal of the Nineteenth Army were by no means full-strength divisions.
2. With these divisions, no front with a width of 200 kilometres would be capable of being held.
3. The front could be regarded as nothing more than a thin line of security.
4. Because of this, the front was bound to be penetrated by any strong enemy attack and would be unable to be held in the long term.
5. For this reason, the request was made to conduct a withdrawal as soon as possible from the line which ran from the plateau of Langres to the Swiss frontier via Dole to a bridgehead position in the vicinity of Belfort. Only then might it be possible for the Nineteenth Army to bring the enemy to a standstill in the Belfort Gap.

The way in which the situation had developed by the end of September confirmed the correctness of the plan that had been proposed by the Nineteenth Army. One crisis led to another, and the defensive strength of the German troops fell rapidly. Even our most outstanding formations could no longer cope with the burden of being committed to action for so long and without pause.

Now that it was the task of the 11th Panzer Division to assume responsibility for the defence of the left wing of the Nineteenth Army on 5 September 1944 in the vicinity of Baume-les-Dames, Montbéliard, Pont-de-Roide, and the Swiss frontier, and to prevent an enemy breakthrough in the direction of Belfort at all costs, its previous role as a mobile and well-equipped formation covering the retreat of the Nineteenth Army across a distance of 450 kilometres came to an end.

The headquarters of the Nineteenth Army and that of the 11th Panzer Division were not always of the same opinion when it came to the employment of the divisional troops. The divisional headquarters sometimes thought too operationally for the army headquarters and, because of this, occasionally needed to be reminded that the panzer division, as a motorised formation, had to secure the route of retreat of the slow-moving Nineteenth Army, whose men had to march on foot. What was most important, however, was that the effective employment of the panzer division would enable the Nineteenth Army to bring as many forces as possible behind the Doubs, thereby preventing the enemy from forcing the Nineteenth Army into a second battle of encirclement, this time in the region of Besançon.

Conclusion

The attacker

The planning for the landing had been worked out in detail in months of staff activity. With excellent cooperation between ground, naval, and air forces, and with the main emphasis being placed on the needs of the ground forces, the landing was carried out systematically.

In the age of atomic weapons, a question that arises is whether the breadth and depth of the landing zone must be expanded significantly to compensate for the wide range of such weapons. If the answer to this question is in the affirmative, the lower levels of command, especially at divisional level, must be given greater freedom of movement and assisted in this regard by the naval units in their combat zones.

Even in the context of the landing on the French southern coast, the conduct of battle by the division which struck in the vicinity of Saint-Raphaël must be regarded as a valuable lesson. Specifically, a regimental group belonging to the division avoided the Gulf of Fréjus entirely due to the strong defensive fire there and swerved around to the north instead.

Airborne landings were to support the seaborne landings and cover the entire periphery of the beachhead to the degree allowed by the situation and the terrain. If the German forces were to be concentrated in one location and prepared to put up significant resistance there, the wide distribution of airborne landings would ensure that most of the airborne units could avoid the danger of being isolated and destroyed.

It had to be taken into consideration that there existed differences between the forces of the various Allied powers when it came to training, equipment, and the conduct of battle. The need for a consistent and united approach was why the first wave of the attack consisted only of American forces.

The means of destruction and construction must be balanced in warfare. More than ever before, ingenious yet structurally simple pioneering techniques are gaining in importance. This study clearly highlights the disastrous situations that could arise if one side or the other was lacking in something like the materiel needed to build or repair a bridge.

Some indication has been given in this book of the significance of the occasionally numerically strong resistance groups of the French Forces of the Interior. A comparison can perhaps be made between the FFI in the Second World War and a territorial defence force today. Has much changed in the importance of such a force for either attacker or defender? A military exercise in France in the autumn of 1964 has established, at least insofar as the results of this exercise have been made public, that the attacker cannot afford to depend too greatly on a territorial defence force being able to hinder the operations of the defender. The fact that territorial defence must be conducted at the expense of the population should not be underestimated psychologically. The primary goal of the population will always be survival.

An attacker who enters a heavily populated country as a liberator must count on the likelihood of multiple delays, as it can be difficult to assess the effect of the enthusiasm of the population on the timetable for the advance. After all, a soldier will not ignore the open arms of the liberated for long.

The defender

Based on the situation report of 12 August 1944, it is natural to assume that the headquarters of the Nineteenth Army may have drawn up plans for the conduct of the retreat, even though the war diaries of the German formations and the personal records of the army chief of staff give no indication – not even a hint – that this was the case. It would have been clear to the army headquarters on the first day of the landing that what had to be done was to save anything that could be saved!

It remains astonishing to this day that no discussions had taken place between the headquarters of Army Group C and that of the Nineteenth Army regarding the coordination of defensive measures in the event of a successful landing by the enemy on the French Mediterranean coast. This fact contributed in no small degree to the development of the battle of encirclement at Montélimar and Loriol, as Army Group C, which was focusing primarily on the protection of its front in the Alps, tied down the 148th and 157th Reserve Divisions to the alpine passes and could therefore do nothing about the gap that had come into existence at Digne.

Marseille and Toulon are clear examples that 'fortresses' have no meaning whatsoever in the age of advanced technology and mobile warfare. The events in Normandy two months earlier proved that such cities were not necessarily of value to the enemy as port towns or transshipment centres. The question therefore remains why the supreme command did not draw the logical conclusions from this. Instead of trying to defend fortress cities, our troops should have destroyed the harbour installations and established defensive lines further inland.

A defender whose combat strength is weaker than that of the attacker only has a chance if he distributes his forces in depth. This was a method which had always been employed successfully by Army Group C and the formations under its command since September 1943. The terrain was just as favourable for defence in southern France as it was in Italy.

Even today, the operations conducted by the 11th Panzer Division would offer a wealth of interesting examples as to how a motorised formation can be employed for flank protection. It would be a highly rewarding exercise to be able to analyse these examples for the purpose of training non-commissioned officers, but the ability to do so is dependent on whether the documents containing the details of the conduct of operations by the panzer division will become available.

Formations and Commanders

German

Nineteenth Army
- Commander: General of Infantry Friedrich Wiese
- Chief of staff: Major-General Botsch
- First general staff officer: Lieutenant-Colonel Schulz
- Senior quartermaster: Colonel Zorn
- Army pioneer commander: Major-General Kaliebe

LXII Reserve Corps
- Commander: General of Infantry Ferdinand Neuling
- Chief of staff: Colonel Meinshagen
- First general staff officer: Major Lademann
- Subordinate formations: 148th Reserve Division (Lieutenant-Colonel Otto Fretter-Pico), 242nd Infantry Division (Lieutenant-General Johannes Baeßler)

LXXXV Army Corps
- Commander: Lieutenant-General Baptist Knieß
- Chief of staff: Colonel Behle
- First general staff officer: Major Becker
- Subordinate formations: 244th Infantry Division (Lieutenant-General Hans Schaefer), 338th Infantry Division (Lieutenant-General René de l'Homme de Courbière)

IV Luftwaffe Field Corps
- Commander: General of Air Troops Erich Petersen
- Chief of staff: Colonel Häring
- First general staff officer: Major Bagdahn
- Subordinate formations: 189th Reserve Division (Colonel Karl Mellwig), 198th Infantry Division (Major-General Otto Schiel), 716th Infantry Division (Lieutenant-General Wilhelm Richter)

The following lower-level formations were either directly subordinate to or assigned to cooperate with the Nineteenth Army.

Directly subordinate: 11th Panzer Division
- Commander: Lieutenant-General Wend von Wietersheim
- First general staff officer: Major Drews

Assigned to cooperate:
- Luftwaffe (2nd Air Division, 5th Flak Brigade)
- Navy (Naval District Southern France, commanded by Vice-Admiral Ernst Scheurlen)

American

US Seventh Army (Lieutenant-General Alexander M. Patch)

US VI Corps
- Commander: Major-General Lucian K. Truscott
- Subordinate formations: US 3rd Infantry Division (Major-General John W. O'Daniel), US 36th Infantry Division (Major-General John E. Dahlquist), US 45th Infantry Division (Major-General William W. Eagles), Allied 1st Airborne Task Force (Major-General Robert T. Frederick)

French

French First Army (Army General Jean de Lattre de Tassigny)
Landing Group I
- French 1st Armoured Division (Divisional General Jean Touzet du Vigier)
- Free French 1st Division (Divisional General Diego Brosset)
- Algerian 3rd Infantry Division (Divisional General Joseph de Goislard de Monsabert)

Landing Group II
- French 9th Colonial Infantry Division (Divisional General Joseph Magnan)
- French 5th Armoured Division (Divisional General Henri de Vernejoul)
- Moroccan 2nd Infantry Division (Divisional General André Dody)
- Moroccan 4th Mountain Division (Divisional General François Sevez)
- Moroccan Tabors (Divisional General Augustin Guillaume)

References

Fighting Forty-Fifth: The Combat Report of an Infantry Division. Baton Rouge, LA: Army & Navy Publishing Company, 1946.

History of the Third Infantry Division in World War II. Washington: Infantry Journal Press, 1947.

Morison, Samuel Eliot, *History of United States Naval Operations in World War II, Volume XI: The Invasion of France and Germany 1944–1945*. Boston: Little, Brown and Company, 1957.

Robichon, Jacques, *Le débarquement de Provence, 15 août 1944*. Paris: Robert Laffont, 1962.

Seventh United States Army Report of Operations in France and Germany 1944–1945, Volume I. Heidelberg: Aloys Gräf, 1946.

Truscott, Lieutenant General Lucian K., *Command Missions: A Personal Story*. New York: E. P. Dutton, 1954.

War diary of the Nineteenth Army with additional documents and situation maps, available from the Federal Military Archives (with neither the documents of the third general staff officer nor those of the senior quartermaster).

Index